Simple Christianity

Rod Loader

BEFORE YOU START

Throughout this book, I refer to many Bible verses. I mainly use the New Living Translation because it is much easier to read and understand, compared to translations like the King James Version, especially for new Christians and people who rarely read Scripture.

I am not going to tell you which Bible translation you should read, through this journey. Some people have very strong opinions on which translation is best. If you have a Bible that you like, please use that, otherwise ask your Pastor, or local Christian bookstore for advice.

Rather than individually name our Heavenly Father, Jesus or the Holy Spirit (or Holy Ghost, as some may prefer) I regularly refer to God. This term only refers to the God of the Bible, the Trinity, where all three are individuals, all three are one and all three are equally worthy of our praise, worship and adoration. No others are truly God.

I want to show how simple Christianity can be.

It is not my way to tell you about this journey and leave you thinking, "I wish I could do that", or "That may be possible for him, but I could never do it".

Instead, my aim is to share what I have learnt from the wonderful journey God has taken me on, so you can build a close, personal and intimate relationship with God, so He can show you how simple Christianity is.

That is why, throughout this book, I give opportunities for us to 'throw off our former ways' and 'renew our thoughts', through four main activities.

__Read__ - taking in information. Which is what you are doing right now.

__Learn__ - looking at God's Word, to find what it says for our lives. We don't need a university degree, or be a pastor, or theologian, to understand the Bible. It was written simply, so we can understand. For those of us, who are not used to looking into what the Bible says, I'll show you some simple methods, so you can see how God's Word can be studied.

__Think__ - considering how we can replace our current ways, with God's ways. The hardest part about this activity is being honest. Sometimes there are things we don't want to admit, even to ourselves. It is important we remember God already knows, and He still loves us deeply.

__Do__ - when we do something about it, which is far less scary than we may think. This will end with a 'Bible Reading' and a 'God Chat'. A God Chat is prayer at its simplest and best. God and us talking quietly and comfortably to each other. At first this may seem strange, even hard, and God may seem distant. We are not used to being in His presence or hearing from Him. Be patient and know He is listening.

Let's start our journey by considering a question I will discuss further in the next section. You can write your answer here, or in a separate journal. The right answer is what you believe right now, not what you think you should write to please me, your pastor, or anyone else.

My walk with God **before** reading this book is _____ because:

_____

After reading, understanding and applying the incredible things God will show us, we will answer the same question again. Your answer may be very different than the one you have written above.

ONLY BELIEVE

"How is your walk with God?"

Have you ever been asked this question? It comes in many forms including, "How's your prayer life?" and "How's your faith life?"

For many years I tried to avoid the question. I would even walk the other way if I heard someone asking that type of question to others.

When I was asked, I would usually respond with something non-comital, like "It's okay". I often added a "thanks", because, as a good Christian, we're supposed to be thankful for questions like that. Aren't we?

In reality "okay" was sometimes a generous estimate. It was no different to how it had been for many years. No better, no worse, but not great.

No, I didn't lie. For thirty years, I tried my best to be a Christian, but I could never understand, or experience, the Christian life described in Matthew 11:28-30.

28Then Jesus said, "Come to me, all of you who are weary and carry heavy burdens, and I will give you rest. 29Take my yoke upon you. Let me teach you, because I am humble and gentle at heart, and you will find rest for your souls. 30For my yoke is easy to bear, and the burden I give you is light."

For thirty years my Christian life was a struggle, I was constantly condemned by sin. I always felt I was never good enough for God, no matter how hard I tried. God always seemed far away. I regularly felt like my prayers hit the ceiling and bounced back at me, as if God rejected them. I remember saying, "If God lets me into Heaven, it will only be at the very outside edge, because I'm not good enough to be close to Him."

I tried different churches, different ways of worship, different activities. I did Worship Leading, Preaching, Youth Group Leadership and being on a start-up church board. I tried different prayer methods and different Bible reading methods. I tried revival meetings, rededicating my life, being prayed for, reading Christian books and a range of other things. Nothing changed. Being a Christian always seemed to be hard work.

Even on the very rare occasion, when God seemed close, I never knew what caused it, or how to make it happen again.

For those that have tried dieting, you might feel the same. Yes, a diet may work for a short while but, too soon, the weight comes back.

My Christian life was the same. It never took long for the weight of life and the burden of my sin to weigh me down again.

In this frame of mind, I felt like I was always failing God. Even though I didn't do any 'terrible' sins, like murder, theft or abusing my family (or others), I still wasn't good enough for God. I felt like every failure was a sin.

Missing a church service was a sin, even though there were days I had to force myself to go. Not praying for an hour was a sin. People like David Yonggi Cho from Korea could pray for hours. HOURS. I barely prayed for a minute (five if I was lucky). Failing to commit to a daily devotional / reading / quiet time was a sin, but many weeks I was lucky if I managed to even open my Bible, even though I did go through periods of serious Bible study it wasn't regular enough.

In short, I did not measure up to the standard 'good' Christians always met. Therefore, I was breaking God rules and sinning. Simple logic. Right?

Wrong!

Many Christians know what John 3:16 says, but do we remember what the next two verses way?

John 3:17-18
[17]God sent his Son into the world not to judge the world, but to save the world through him.

[18]"There is no judgment against anyone who believes in him. But anyone who does not believe in him has already been judged for not believing in God's one and only Son.

So, if Jesus did not come to judge me and there is no judgment for anyone who believes in Jesus, why did I feel constantly judged?

Hint: It's not God.

This is exactly what our enemy does. Yes, we have an enemy. An enemy that wants us so focused on trying to be a 'perfect' Christian (or even a 'good' Christian) and so bound by guilt, for failing to meet those unrealistic expectations, that we miss the only version of Christianity God wants for us. The simple version.

God's desire is for Christianity to be simple. It was never meant to be difficult. In Mark 10:15 Jesus says, *"I tell you the truth, anyone who doesn't receive the Kingdom of God like a child will never enter it"*.

Matthew 18:2-4 says, *[2]Jesus called a little child to him and put the child among them. [3]Then he said, "I tell you the truth, unless you turn from your sins and become like little children, you will never get into the Kingdom of Heaven. [4]So anyone who becomes as humble as this little child is the greatest in the Kingdom of Heaven.*

Why did Jesus use a child as an example? Because children see things simply. They love, they accept and they trust. They only question to understand, never to doubt.

Children are taught (or forced) to hate, to reject, to distrust and to stop asking questions. This was never God's plan for them, or for us as His children.

Senior Pastor George Miller once told me how to live God's way. He summed it up in two words, "Only Believe". This is the simplest, most accurate, most profound explanation I have heard. It is also the hardest.

It is the simplest as it has only two words. It is the most accurate, as it is exactly what God wants us to do. It is the most profound, as the more we think about it, the more it forces us to dive deep, to understanding God and His Word. It is the hardest because it is exactly the opposite of what our human nature, and our enemy, the devil, demands.

The reason these words are all these things is because, as Pastor George freely admits, they are the words of Jesus, as recorded in Mark 5:36 and Luke 8:50.

The Simplest
Jesus always had an ability to simplify the most complicated issues.

Mark 5:21-43 and Luke 8:40-56 tell of the time when Jairus, a synagogue leader, came to Jesus. Jairus' daughter was ill, and he asked Jesus to heal her. While Jairus was talking to Jesus, Jairus was told his daughter had died. It was then Jesus said the words "Only believe".

He didn't ask for a perfect history, he didn't say, "You're a synagogue leader (equivalent to a pastor, or priest). You should know." He didn't check if there was regular attendance at church, or home group, or prayer group, or any other group. No. He saw a need and He asked for the simple thing God wants us to do. Believe.

Most Accurate
It was the most accurate because it is exactly what God wants us to do. Before we think, believe. Before we act, believe. In the Bible, this is called having faith.

Hebrews 11 gives examples of people who had faith and had their faith rewarded.
By faith, Abel brought a more acceptable offering to God than Cain did (v4).
By faith, Enoch was taken up to heaven without dying (v5).
By faith, Noah built a large boat to save his family from the flood (v7).
By faith, Abraham obeyed when God called him to … go to another land (v8).

By faith, Sarah was able to have a child, though she was barren and was too old (v11).

Most Profound
It is the most profound because it represents the foundation of Christianity, which is to 'have faith'.

Hebrews chapter 11, verses 1, 3 and 6 state this clearly.

[1]Faith shows the reality of what we hope for; it is the evidence of things we cannot see.

[3]By faith we understand that the entire universe was formed at God's command, that what we now see did not come from anything that can be seen.

[6]And it is impossible to please God without faith. Anyone who wants to come to him must believe that God exists and that he rewards those who sincerely seek him.

The Hardest
It is the hardest because we are not involved in making it happen. Often, we want to do something, or say something, to make it happen. Believing requires we let God be in total control and we 'Only Believe'.

It is this response Jesus sought each time He healed, raise the dead and even calmed the storm.

Immediately after calming the storm, in Luke 8:24, Jesus chastises the disciples (verse 25). He wasn't disappointed because they didn't give their tithe that week, or attend both Sunday morning and night services, but because they did not believe.

Both the Old and the New Testaments have many examples, like this, where God is telling us to only believe.

Learn
Read Mark 5:21-43 and Luke 8:40-56 and write how the different people reacted.

Jairus

_____

The mourners

_____

The Disciples

Jesus

Think
If you had a similar situation today and were told to "Only Believe", how would you react? Be honest. Your answer does not have to please me, or your pastor. It is just you and God.

How is this different to how Jesus wanted Jairus to think and act?

Do
Over the next few days, use the term "Only Believe" as often as possible, applying it to different situations. This will reinforce what God says about standing in faith.

Bible reading
Read John 14:1, John 20:31, 1 Thessalonians 4:14, 1John 5:13

These passages tell us about believing in Jesus and God. Believing without physical evidence is faith. This is a major way we show God, we trust Him.

Our feelings can deceive us, especially if we are relying on them to tell us if God is working. When we are reading God's Word, or talking with God, and we have negative feelings, ignore those feelings, and have certainty God is working in our hearts and communicating with us, through the Holy Spirit.

God chat
Tell God what it means to you, to know He wants you to 'Only believe'. Please remember this is a chat with God, which can be as casual, or formal, as you desire. He is listening and He will respond, we only need to tune our radios to hear Him, which is done when we 'Only Believe'.

IDENTITY

Part 1- What God Really Thinks of Me

When we think of God, how do we imagine Him? Is He distant, cold and angry, or close, inviting and loving?

Before we can begin to experience the life God wants for us, it is very important we have the correct understanding of what God thinks of us, which directly affects what we think of God.

How we see God determines how we read the Bible, which is God's Word for us. Too often we have an incorrect, or poor, concept of what God thinks of us. This affects every word we read.

If we had a distant or abusive earthly father, and we read (or are told) God is our Heavenly Father, then we read any of the multiple passages where God judges people, especially in the Old Testament, this will only reinforce that negative image of God.

There are many churches, that strongly emphasize God's judgement and man's sinful nature. As a result, God's deep and endless love for us can be under-emphasized. I understand why this is done. Man's nature is sinful. 1John 1:8 says, *If we claim we have no sin, we are only fooling ourselves and not living in the truth.*

However, sin cannot be overcome by constantly reminding us of our failures. Sin is overcome when we desire the life God has for us, more than the one we are living.

Far too often, we believe our life as Christians starts and ends with work we are to do, like Discipleship, Evangelism, Serving and even Loving. Loving is a work, sometimes the hardest work. Yet, the life God wants for us does not start with works. Instead, it starts with knowing what God thinks of us (Identity), moves to how we are to react to that (Worship), then to the wonderful working power of God (Miracles), before finishing with how we can tell others about the life God wants for all of us (Sharing).

This ensures each of us builds a relationship with God, so we know Him personally, a strange concept for many Christians, long before learning how to share with others.

That is why the first part of our journey starts with our identity.

Our identity is how God sees us. We need to understand, in our heart, not just our head, how much God loves us, how much He has done for us and how special we are to Him.

Our identity is the foundation on which all other learning must be built, because our identity starts before the earth was made, goes through the cross and ends at eternity with our Heavenly Father.

What God says to me.
God loves each of us more deeply than we can know or imagine. He longs to have a loving Father / child relationship with us. He thinks we (including you) are so wonderful He wants to live in us now and be with us forever.

Even when we struggle with faith, or miss church services, or continue in a sin we know we should not do, or even deny Jesus because we are threatened with death, we can still know, with absolute certainty, God will always love us and never let us go.

I don't make this claim because I want you to feel good. This is a truth from God's Word and God does not lie. He will never repeat the lies the world tells us. He tells us the truth about who we are and what He thinks about us.

Hebrews 6:18 says, *So God has given both his promise and his oath. These two things are unchangeable because it is impossible for God to lie.*

Numbers 23:19 says, *God is not a man, so he does not lie. He is not human, so he does not change his mind.*

Let's look at some Bible passages and understand the wonderful things God says to us, and what He has done for all of us who have accepted Jesus as Savior and Lord. (I'll discuss more about Jesus, as our Savior and Lord soon.)

Ephesians 1:3-8
God says, "I have richly blessed you."
3All praise to God, the Father of our Lord Jesus Christ, who has blessed us with every spiritual blessing in the heavenly realms because we are united with Christ.

God says, "I have loved you from the very beginning. You are blameless in my eyes."
4Even before he made the world, God loved us and chose us in Christ to be holy and without fault in his eyes.

God says, "I am very happy to make you part of my family."
5God decided in advance to adopt us into his own family by bringing us to himself through Jesus Christ. This is what he wanted to do, and it gave him great pleasure.

God says, "I have covered you with the gift of my amazing grace."
⁶So we praise God for the glorious grace he has poured out on us who belong to his dear Son.

God says, "I wanted to pay the price, to set you free from a life that leads to death."
⁷He is so rich in kindness and grace that he purchased our freedom with the blood of his Son and forgave our sins.

God says, "I give you my kindness, wisdom and understanding."
⁸He has showered his kindness on us, along with all wisdom and understanding.

Psalms 9:9-10
God says, "I am your refuge in hard times."
⁹The LORD is a shelter for the oppressed, a refuge in times of trouble.

God says, "I will never abandon you."
¹⁰Those who know your name trust in you, for you, O LORD, do not abandon those who search for you.

Psalm 139:16-17
God says, "Before you were born, I had a wonderful plan for you."
¹⁶You saw me before I was born. Every day of my life was recorded in your book. Every moment was laid out before a single day had passed.

God says, "I think about you very often."
¹⁷How precious are your thoughts about me, O God. They cannot be numbered!

Learn
From the passages above, write things God has done for you.

_____

_____

_____

_____

Think
Knowing God says these things about you. How does it make you feel?

_____

_____

Do

For the next seven days, read these verses aloud. This will reinforce what God says about you.

Bible reading
Read Ephesians chapter 1, pausing very regularly, to allow God to tell you about His love for you. Initially this may be a feeling of love, peace or joy, when we are reading, or thinking about what we have read.

Although our feelings can deceive us, especially if we are relying on them to tell us if God is working, not all feelings are incorrect. The fruit of God's Spirit (the Holy Spirit) is love, joy, peace, patience, kindness, goodness, faithfulness, gentleness and self-control. When we are reading God's Word, or talking with God, and we have these feelings, we can have certainty God is working in our hearts and communicating with us, through the Holy Spirit.

Very few of us will hear God speak. Some hear thoughts that align with God's nature or Word, but most of us, especially to start, will sense God's Spirit working as I just described.

God chat
Tell God what it means to you, to know He loves you.

What God says I am.

Even when we make mistakes, we can know God has already seen every sin we will ever do, and still wants us. Deuteronomy 4:31 says, *For the LORD your God is a merciful God; He will not abandon you or destroy you or forget the covenant with your fathers, which He swore to them by oath.*

1 Samuel 12:22 says, *The LORD will not abandon his people, because that would dishonor his great name. For it has pleased the LORD to make you his very own people.*

That doesn't mean we can keep sinning and get away with it. That is called False Grace, or Hyper Grace, and is not acceptable to God. I'll discuss this more in the section on Worship.

It does mean God's love for us is unchanging. It also means there is nothing we can do to make him love us more. His decision to love us was decided long before we were born. It was confirmed the moment Jesus shed His blood and died for us.

That is why we can read the things God says about us, knowing they will not change.

Here are some of the many wonderful truths about us.

I am created in God's image.
Genesis 1:27
So God created human beings in his own image. In the image of God he created them; male and female he created them.

I am one of God's people.
1 Peter 2:9-10
⁹But you are not like that, for you are a chosen people. You are royal priests, a holy nation, God's very own possession. As a result, you can show others the goodness of God, for he called you out of the darkness into his wonderful light. ¹⁰"Once you had no identity as a people; now you are God's people. Once you received no mercy; now you have received God's mercy."

Also read Psalm 100:3 and John 15:5

I am made by God.
Psalm 139:13-16
¹³You made all the delicate, inner parts of my body and knit me together in my mother's womb. ¹⁴Thank you for making me so wonderfully complex! Your workmanship is marvelous—how well I know it. ¹⁵You watched me as I was being formed in utter seclusion, as I was woven together in the dark of the womb.

[16]You saw me before I was born. Every day of my life was recorded in your book. Every moment was laid out before a single day had passed.

Also read Isaiah 64:8 and Ephesians 2:10

I have been set free by God, who paid the price for my freedom.
Romans 3:24-26
[24]Yet God, with undeserved kindness, declares that we are righteous. He did this through Christ Jesus when he freed us from the penalty for our sins.
[25]For God presented Jesus as the sacrifice for sin. People are made right with God when they believe that Jesus sacrificed his life, shedding his blood. This sacrifice shows that God was being fair when he held back and did not punish those who sinned in times past, [26]for he was looking ahead and including them in what he would do in this present time. God did this to demonstrate his righteousness, for he himself is fair and just, and he declares sinners to be right in his sight when they believe in Jesus.

Also read Isaiah 43:1 and 1 Corinthians 6:20

God knows me personally and I am special to Him.
Isaiah 43:1-3
[1]Do not be afraid, for I have ransomed you. I have called you by name; you are mine. [2]When you go through deep waters, I will be with you. When you go through rivers of difficulty, you will not drown. When you walk through the fire of oppression, you will not be burned up; the flames will not consume you. [3]For I am the LORD, your God, the Holy One of Israel, your Savior.

Also read Isaiah 49:16, Jeremiah 1:5, Matthew 6:26, Ephesians 2:4-5, 13 &19

I am His temple.
1 Corinthians 6:19-20
[19]Do you not know that your body is a temple of the Holy Spirit who is in you, whom you have received from God? You are not your own; [20]you were bought at a price. Therefore glorify God with your body.

Also read 1Corinthians 3:16-17 and 1Peter 2:5

I am a child of God.
John 1:12
But to all who believed him and accepted him, he gave the right to become children of God.

Also read Romans 8:14-17, Galatians 3:26 & 29, Ephesians 1:11 & 13-14 and Philippians 3:20

As you will have noticed, none of these are negative. Unlike the world, which brings us down, God only wants to lift us up, by constantly showing us how special and important we are to Him.

Learn
After reading these verses, do you believe God is distant, cold and angry, or close, inviting and loving? Why?

_____

_____

Think
Knowing you are all these things to God, what things could you do differently?

_____

_____

Do
Reread these verses aloud and say who you are, proclaiming it as the truth it is. You can say something like this: "I am not what the world says, I am a child of God." Then read the appropriate verses.

Bible reading
Read Isaiah chapter 54, pausing regularly, to allow God to tell you about how He cares for you.

God chat
Thank God for all the ways he loves you. Ask Him to show you more ways that He loves you.

The Bible is filled with verses like these. The more time we spend reading the Bible, the more God will show us. That is one wonderful reason why we need to spend time in God's Word.

A great place to start reading the Bible is Ephesians, then Philippians, then Colossians. These books are similar in message, are next to each other and are quite short, so they are good if you are not used to reading the Bible. After that the Gospel of John gives a wonderful image of Jesus.

Now we have gained an understanding of who God says we are, it is time to look at how we build a relationship with God.

IDENTITY

Part 2 - What God Wants Me to Be

Now we have spent time looking at what God thinks of us, it is important to understand what God wants us to be.

He wants us to be His children. He wants us to build a close and personal relationship with Him. He wants us to be a part of what He is doing.

In the last section, we read passages stating the things God has done for us, but they also say these things are 'in Christ', or 'through Christ', or because of what Jesus has done.

This includes:
Ephesians 1:4-7
4Even before he made the world, God loved us and chose us in Christ to be holy and without fault in his eyes. 5God decided in advance to adopt us into his own family by bringing us to himself through Jesus Christ. This is what he wanted to do, and it gave him great pleasure. 6So we praise God for the glorious grace he has poured out on us who belong to his dear Son. 7He is so rich in kindness and grace that he purchased our freedom with the blood of his Son and forgave our sins.

Some of us may be asking what this has to do with having a relationship with God. The answer is everything. Long before we even knew about God, He loved us. Even when we hate God, or refuse to believe in Him, God still loves us and everything He says about us still applies.

However, when we are living sinful lives, our sin keeps us separated from God. Sin is doing what we want, instead of what God wants. Sin keeps us separated from God because, when we sin, our focus and desire is on things other than God. Sin puts us as the most important part of our lives, instead of God, who made us, loves us deeply and has a wonderful life for us.

Some of us honestly believe we can be right with God (righteous) by trying to live a 'good' life. If we do more good things than bad things, God will give us a place in Heaven. Others believe if we obey all God's rules, we will earn His favour and an eternity with God. These beliefs assume our efforts (our 'works') can make us acceptable to God.

The Bible is very specific about our ability to earn our way into Heaven, or into God's favour.

Romans 3:23

for all have sinned and fall short of the glory of God. (NASB)

Romans 4:2
If his good deeds had made him acceptable to God, he would have had something to boast about. But that was not God's way.

Titus 3:4-5
⁴When God our Savior revealed his kindness and love, ⁵he saved us, not because of the righteous things we had done, but because of his mercy.

If, through our efforts, we can't earn our way into God's favour, what are we to do?

Even Jesus' disciples asked, "Who then can be saved?" Matthew 19:25 (NKJV)

Fortunately, Jesus' response gives us all hope.
"With men this is impossible, but with God all things are possible." Matthew 19:26 (NKJV)

Jesus' response refers to the Good News, that applies to us all.

What Is the Good News?
The Good News tells us what God has done, so we can have a relationship with Him.

1. God Loves Us
Since the beginning of time God has wanted a deep, personal relationship with each of us, based on love not rules. This love is unchanging, just as God is unchanging.

Ephesians 1:4-5 (The book of Ephesians, chapter 1, verses 4 to 5) says:
⁴Even before he made the world, God loved us and chose us in Christ to be holy and without fault in his eyes. ⁵God decided in advance to adopt us into his own family by bringing us to himself through Jesus Christ. This is what he wanted to do, and it gave him great pleasure.

It is this love we have read and learnt about, in the first part of this book.

2. We Have Sinned
Since Adam and Eve chose to obey the devil, instead of God, our natural tendency has been to disobey God. We want to be the 'boss' of our own lives. This causes us to sin.

Romans 3:10-12 describes the natural tendencies of people.

[10]As the Scriptures say, "No one is righteous—not even one. [11]No one is truly wise; no one is seeking God. [12]All have turned away; all have become useless. No one does good, not a single one."

Verse 23 in the same chapter summarizes with:
For everyone has sinned; we all fall short of God's glorious standard.

Romans 8:7-8 explains why our sinful nature can never please God.
[7]For the sinful nature is always hostile to God. It never did obey God's laws, and it never will. [8]That's why those who are still under the control of their sinful nature can never please God.

3. Sin Brings Punishment
Although God is a loving God, He is also a just God, which means He cannot allow sin to remain unpunished. Whether we have done one sin, or a million sins, the punishment is the same. This punishment, also called 'death', is eternal separation from God, in a place where there is no love, joy, peace, patience, kindness or gentleness. This place is called Hell.

The following passages, from the Bible, give examples of how God punishes those who sin.

Matthew 13:41-42
[41]The Son of Man will send his angels, and they will remove from his Kingdom everything that causes sin and all who do evil. [42]And the angels will throw them into the fiery furnace, where there will be weeping and gnashing of teeth.

Romans 6:16
Don't you realize that you become the slave of whatever you choose to obey? You can be a slave to sin, which leads to death, or you can choose to obey God, which leads to righteous living.

Romans 8:5-6 describes the result of our sinful nature.
[5]Those who are dominated by the sinful nature think about sinful things, but those who are controlled by the Holy Spirit think about things that please the Spirit. [6]So letting your sinful nature control your mind leads to death. But letting the Spirit control your mind leads to life and peace.

Also read 2Peter 2:4-6 and Romans 6:23.

Every person has sinned, no one is free from sin. In our own strength and abilities, we are unable to escape punishment for the sin we have done. Fortunately, God knew this and had a plan to save us. That plan was Jesus.

4. God Sent Jesus

God never wants anyone to go to Hell. He knew there was no way we can become right with God through our own efforts, for committing one sin in our entire lives would make us fail. Therefore, He sent His only Son, Jesus, to take our punishment.

As Jesus is God in human form, he committed no sin, but he died on the cross for all the sin we have done and will ever do. This death satisfied God's requirements, allowing us to become right with God.

Romans 8:3-4

³The law of Moses was unable to save us because of the weakness of our sinful nature. So, God did what the law could not do. He sent his own Son in a body like the bodies we sinners have. And in that body God declared an end to sin's control over us by giving his Son as a sacrifice for our sins. ⁴He did this so that the just requirement of the law would be fully satisfied for us, who no longer follow our sinful nature but instead follow the Spirit.

Romans 3:24-26

²⁴Yet God, with undeserved kindness, declares that we are righteous. He did this through Christ Jesus when he freed us from the penalty for our sins. ²⁵For God presented Jesus as the sacrifice for sin. People are made right with God when they believe that Jesus sacrificed his life, shedding his blood. This sacrifice shows that God was being fair when he held back and did not punish those who sinned in times past, ²⁶for he was looking ahead and including them in what he would do in this present time. God did this to demonstrate his righteousness, for he himself is fair and just, and he declares sinners to be right in his sight when they believe in Jesus.

Also read John 3:16-17

The first decision we need to make, is to believe Jesus died, as the sacrifice God required for our past, present and future sins. We need to have faith God did this for us. Faith is not hope, it is certainty. This is known as 'accepting Jesus as our Savior'.

When we do this, we are covered by the sacrifice Jesus made and all our sins will be washed away, setting us free.

5. We Repent

Repent means to 'change our focus'. Repenting is not a desire. It is an action. We are to turn from sin-based thinking and living, putting Jesus in control, as the Lord (owner) of our lives. Nothing less. This is full-time commitment, not part-time following. We are to give up our lives, our goals, our dreams, even our thoughts, to do what God tells us, as Jesus did. Recently, I saw a quote on a church notice board, which states this very well. It said, "God wants full time custody, not weekend visits."

As God loves us so much, He gives us all the years we have on this earth, to choose to accept Jesus as Savior and Lord. If we refuse to do this, God will respect our choice and never force His will on us. However, when we physically die, we must then face the punishment for all our sins. Which is to be eternally separated from God because God cannot allow sin in Heaven. Therefore, we will spend an eternity in Hell. God does not send us to Hell. By refusing to accept Jesus, we choose Hell.

Let me give an example:
A man wanted to kill people. He knew it was against the law and carried a punishment. He still bought a gun, then killed several people. He was arrested and brought before a judge. The judge sentenced him to life in prison. Was it the judge that condemned the man, or was it the man's choices and actions?

It was the man's choices and actions that resulted in the prison sentence. The judge only stated the result of the man's choices. The decision given by God, to send people to Hell, is a direct result of people's choices and actions.

God's Word talks about this choice a lot, including theses passages.

Romans 6:12-14
¹²Do not let sin control the way you live; do not give in to sinful desires. ¹³Do not let any part of your body become an instrument of evil to serve sin. Instead, give yourselves completely to God, for you were dead, but now you have new life. So, use your whole body as an instrument to do what is right for the glory of God. ¹⁴Sin is no longer your master, for you no longer live under the requirements of the law. Instead, you live under the freedom of God's grace.

John 5:24
²⁴"I tell you the truth, those who listen to my message and believe in God who sent me have eternal life. They will never be condemned for their sins, but they have already passed from death into life.

Romans 8:1-2
¹So now there is no condemnation for those who belong to Christ Jesus. ²And because you belong to him, the power of the life-giving Spirit has freed you from the power of sin that leads to death.

When death is mentioned in passages about eternal life, it means eternal separation from God. Which is hell.

6. Relationship

When we give our lives completely to Jesus, making Him Lord of our lives, God creates a new spirit in us. This is called Born Again. Being Born Again is not a theoretical idea, it happens. People are changed, they think and act differently. I have spoken to many Christians who share about the dramatic way God changed them, always for the better.

God also sends His Holy Spirit to live in us. The Holy Spirit helps us to build the relationship with God, allowing us to see Him as loving father, even calling him Abba, which means Dad.

Romans 8:14-16
[14]For all who are led by the Spirit of God are children of God. [15]So you have not received a spirit that makes you fearful slaves. Instead, you received God's Spirit when he adopted you as his own children. Now we call him, "Abba, Father." [16]For his Spirit joins with our spirit to affirm that we are God's children.

Romans 5:1-2
[1]Therefore, since we have been made right in God's sight by faith, we have peace with God because of what Jesus Christ our Lord has done for us. [2]Because of our faith, Christ has brought us into this place of undeserved privilege where we now stand, and we confidently and joyfully look forward to sharing God's glory.

Learn
What does each part of the Good News mean to you? Why?

_____

_____

_____

_____

_____

Think
How does knowing what God has done, to have a relationship with you, change how you see God?

_____

_____

Do
Look at the life you are living. Is it fully committed to Jesus? List areas you need to turn from (repent). This may be difficult as we may have kept many of these things secret.

_____

_____

_____

Bible reading
Read Romans chapter 8 and Ephesians chapter 2, pausing regularly, to allow God to show you the truth of what He has done for you.

God chat
Look at the list of areas you have written. Now confess them to God, asking Him to help you to turn from those things. You DON'T need a priest or pastor to do this. You have full access to God. Hebrews 4:16 says, *So let us come boldly to the throne of our gracious God. There we will receive his mercy, and we will find grace to help us when we need it most.*

When we confess our areas of error (our sins), even if it is only to God, we have made the first important step in turning from them (repenting). God will show us mercy and grace to help us.

When we sin, which we all will, God will convict us. This is always a loving, and often gentle, reminder we are doing things, that are not part of the life He has for us. He will NEVER condemn, belittle or attack us. If we feel this way, it is not God, it is the devil.

In John 10:10 Jesus says, *"The thief comes only to steal and kill and destroy; I came that they may have life, and have it abundantly"*. (NASB)

The devil wants us to feel condemned and unworthy of God's love and grace, so we focus on our sin instead of God. We are to resist (disobey) the devil and seek God all the time.

Being A Child of God

Now we know what God loves each of us and wants a loving relationship with us, we can approach God from the perspective that He wants to love and care for us. Knowing this, we will be far more willing to listen to Him and do what He asks.

Romans 8:38-39
38I am convinced that nothing can ever separate us from God's love. Neither death nor life, neither angels nor demons, neither our fears for today nor our worries about tomorrow—not even the powers of hell can separate us from God's love. 39No power in the sky above or in the earth below—indeed, nothing in all creation will ever be able to separate us from the love of God that is revealed in Christ Jesus our Lord.

If we can never be separated from God's love and God wants us as His children, how can I be the child God wants me to be? More than anything else God wants our time. We can't build a relationship with a person if we never spend time with them. The same applies to God.

See God as our Father, far better than any earthly father.
It doesn't matter if your earthly father was non-existent, poor or wonderful, God is far better than they could ever be. God wants us to see Him as our Father because that is what He is.

When we give our lives to Jesus, God creates a new spirit in us, a spirit from Him, making us spiritually Born Again. God is the one who has given us new life, on this earth, and eternally with Him. That is why He wants us to call Him Father, or Dad, even Daddy, because He wants intimacy not distance.

Ephesians 1:5
He decided we would be adopted as sons, through Jesus, and this brought Him pleasure.

1John 3:1
See how very much our Father loves us, for he calls us his children, and that is what we are! But the people who belong to this world don't recognize that we are God's children because they don't know him.

Give up our lives to do what God want us to do
God has wonderful plans for our lives, these plans are far better than anything we can plan. That is why God wants us to release control of our lives, plans, hopes and dreams, to allow Him to show us a better way to live, and better things to do.

1Corinthians 15:58
So, my dear brothers and sisters, be strong and immovable. Always work enthusiastically for the Lord, for you know that nothing you do for the Lord is ever useless.

John 12:26
Anyone who wants to be my disciple must follow me, because my servants must be where I am. And the Father will honor anyone who serves me.

It is important we spend time seeking God, to know what He wants us to do. We can spend all our lives doing things 'for God', but never actually do what He wants us to do. This leads to resentment, frustration and burnout.

Instead, as we grow closer to God, He will show us what He wants us to do. When He gives us tasks, very often they will be beyond our capabilities. This is not to cause us stress or pain, but to make us realize we cannot do it on our own, we are always to rely completely on Him.

Seek God with all our heart.
We seek God by calling out to Him and having a heart attitude of seeking God before anything else.

Matthew 6:33
seek first the kingdom of God and His righteousness (being right in God's sight).

Matthew 5:6
blessed are those who hunger and thirst for righteousness, for they shall be filled.

God wants us to search for Him the same as we'd search for food or drink, after several days without them. Hungering and thirsting are the levels of yearning God wants us to have for Him, throughout our Christian life.

God does not need us to do this, he allows us to do it, so we understand He wants us to always have this level of seeking Him, far above all other things. The more we do this, the more God helps us to grow closer and closer to Him.

Seeking God is done in three main ways. Although we need to do all three, they do not need to be done together, or in any specific order.

1. Read God's Word. This is how we learn from Him. His Word gives us all the instructions and guidance we need throughout our lives. This is also the most common way He will communicate to many of us.

2. Talk with God. This is how we communicate to Him. He is always interested and always listens. Never think your prayers don't get through. Although some of us will hear Him respond, many of us may only get an answer through the actions or words of others, or through reading the Bible.

3. Spend time with God. This is spending periods of time alone with God, with no distractions. This can be anything from a few minutes to many hours, asking

God to help us to be closer to Him. This can be hard, as our world is full of distractions, but it is often the most rewarding.

For me spending time alone with God is my favourite time, as I feel God's presence. I know the idea of 'feeling' God's presence is a strange concept for many of us. Consider this: occasionally we may have had a church service that was far better, more uplifting, perhaps even more holy, than others. During these times we felt closer to God. We may have even had a pastor, or elder, say, "God was here, today." That is the feeling of God's presence. As I explained earlier, we must never rely on our feelings, to know God is present, we can have absolute faith He is. But when He makes His presence felt, it is amazing.

Learn
How does Romans 8:38-39 and 1John 3:1 above, change your reason for seeking more of God?

_____

_____

_____

Think
What could you do to draw closer to God?

_____

_____

Do
Each day for the next week, seek God in all three ways listed above.

Bible reading
Read Colossians chapters 2 and 3.

God chat
Talk to God about all the ways He has shown you who you are. Spend at least 10 minutes (longer if possible) with God, asking Him to come closer, then waiting for Him to respond.

The Next Step

As Christians, we can rush from conversion (accepting Jesus) to works (doing things for God). Too often, this is without gaining a good, or any, understanding of what God thinks of us, who God says we are and how to have a relationship with God.

Yet God repeatedly tells us how much He loves us and what He has done for us, so we can be close to Him. It is God's promises about us and his actions for us, that need to be the foundation of our Christian life.

When we understand that God willingly sent His Son, Jesus, to die for us, so we can become God's children, we start to see Christianity is not a burden. In fact, it is the opposite. It is a loving relationship with our Heavenly Father, who chose us before He created the world.

Our identity is not, and never should be, based on what we do, what we think of ourselves, or what others say about us. Our identity must be based on what God says about us. It is He who gives us worth, for we are worth the life of Jesus. This worth (value) can never be taken from us by anyone on this earth, or the devil, because they never gave it to us.

At a Men's Camp people were introducing themselves to the group. Men would stand, give their name, then their profession. This is how we are identified in the world, by what we do. When my turn came, I said, "I'm Rod and I'm a child of God." I did this to share my identity from God's perspective. It can be little actions like this, that help others see who God says they are.

Only God honestly tells us who we are. God sets our identity. It is wonderful that the Creator of the universe calls us His child. This can take some time to sink into our hearts. Allow yourself to take that time. You will see God, and yourself, very differently. When this begins to happen, you will be ready to move onto the next wonderful part of our journey.

Worship.

WORSHIP

Part 1 - What Worship Is

When we think of worship, what springs to mind? Is it singing on a Sunday morning? Or an attitude when we approach God? Or even something we do?

For many years I believed worship comprised of three main areas, doing things for God, saying how good God is and singing worship songs. How worshipful was I when I sang Amazing Grace? I was doing all three things.

What I did not understand at the time, was I could do all three things and still not worship God.

Outside the church, worship is often an expression of reverence, adoration or devotion toward a god, person or principle.

In the world this is true, as worship is about admiring or desiring to be like people, whether they be sport stars, movie stars or musicians, and desiring things like money and fame.

In the first portion of this book, we looked at our identity. As we discovered, our identity is based on what God says we are, rather than what people say. The same applies to worship.

Therefore, regarding worship, the most important question is not, "What do we want worship to be?" Instead, it is, "What does God want worship to be?"

Before we look at what worship should be, we need to look at what worship should not be. It is important we start here, as we can have incorrect ideas about worship, that need to be cleared away, before our minds and hearts can focus on the beautiful, and inspiring, thing God calls 'Worship'.

What Worship Is Not

Worship is not - about us.
This may sound like an obvious statement. We worship God, not ourselves, right?

It would be wonderful if that was always the case, unfortunately the world in which we live is strongly focused on worshiping ourselves.

Think about the advertisements we see. They almost scream, "You will be noticed, if you drive this car", or "You will be loved, if you chew this gum or use this deodorant". The world wants us to focus on attention of ourselves, to lavish praise on ourselves and to put ourselves above all others. Regardless of what we may like to call it, that is worshiping ourselves.

Jesus noticed people were doing the same thing, and he spoke strongly against it.

Matthew 6:1-6
Don't do your good deeds publicly, to be admired by others (verse 1)
Give your gifts in private (verse 4)
When you pray, don't be like the hypocrites who love to pray (verse 5)
But when you pray, go away by yourself, shut the door behind you, and pray to your Father in private (verse 6)

Matthew 6:16 says, *When you fast, don't make it obvious, as the hypocrites do, for they try to look miserable ... so people will admire them for their fasting.*

The people Jesus was talking about here were not worldly people, or new Christians. No, these were the Pharisees, the leaders of the church, the people who should be setting the example for Godly living. Instead, they were seeking glory for themselves. They were seeking to be admired, to be revered, to be worshiped.

This behaviour never pleases God, even if we try to justify it by saying, "we are doing God's work". That is why Jesus said, "they have received all the reward they will ever get."

This does not mean we must hide in a closet all the time, so others will never notice us. When we live the life God has for us, we will be noticed by others.

Matthew 5:14-16 says:
[14]"You are the light of the world. A city set on a hill cannot be hidden; [15]nor does anyone light a lamp and put it under a basket, but on the lampstand, and it gives light to all who are in the house. [16]"Let your light shine before men in such a way that they may see your good works, and glorify your Father who is in heaven. (NASB)

For many of us, only a few will notice us, for some it will be far more public.

Desiring to be worshiped is not about how public our actions are, it is about a heart attitude. A desire to seek the focus of others, to seek glory for ourselves, rather than direct attention to the only one who rightly deserves all worship.

The Bible is very specific about who deserves all worship.

2Kings 17:35-36
35b *"Do not worship any other gods or bow down to them, serve them or sacrifice to them. 36But the Lord, who brought you up out of Egypt with mighty power and outstretched arm, is the one you must worship.* (NIV)

Matthew 4:10
Then Jesus said to him, "Away with you, Satan! For it is written, 'You shall worship the LORD your God, and Him only you shall serve.'" (NKJV)

Neither of these verses, or the many more that talk about worshiping, say worship is about drawing attention to ourselves. However, many talk about the consequences of worshiping anyone, or anything, other than God.

In Mark 4:19, Jesus talks about making anything in our lives more important than God, when He says, *"but the worries of the world, and the deceitfulness of riches, and the desires for other things enter in and choke the word, and it becomes unfruitful."* (NASB)

When anything, or anyone, is more important than God, we restrict the effectiveness of God's work and Word in our lives. We can't restrict God. That's impossible. But when our hearts and minds are focused on anything other than God, we no longer focus on what He wants us to do. This results in us becoming unfruitful.

Worship is not about us. It never was and never should be.

Learn
From the two passages from Matthew, above, list the specific actions Jesus spoke against.

_____

_____

_____

Think
Are there any of these actions in your life right now?

List any areas of your life you are putting ahead of God.

A simple measure is: If you would rather focus on someone or something rather than God, then it is more important to you than God.

_____

_____

_____

_____

_Do_
Write any ways you could direct glory to God rather than yourself.

_____

_____

_____

_____

_____

Bible reading
Read Matthew chapter 23. This passage discusses the Pharisee's behaviours and the consequences of those actions.

God chat
Talk to God about areas of your life that you are putting ahead of Him. Ask God to help you focus on Him instead.

Worship is not - about activities.

Like many of us, I used to believe doing God's work was one way of putting God first. Therefore, I was worshiping Him.

In Matthew 5:16, Jesus says, *"Let your light shine before men in such a way that they may see your good works, and glorify your Father who is in heaven."* (NASB)

Based on this, and similar verses, we can easily believe doing good things, or good works will bring glory to God. So did the Israelites in the Old Testament. Yet, in Isaiah, God said these words.

Isaiah 1:11-15
[11]"The multitude of your sacrifices—
what are they to me?" says the Lord.
"I have more than enough of burnt offerings,
of rams and the fat of fattened animals;
I have no pleasure
in the blood of bulls and lambs and goats.
[12]When you come to appear before me,
who has asked this of you,
this trampling of my courts?
[13]Stop bringing meaningless offerings!
Your incense is detestable to me.
New Moons, Sabbaths and convocations—
I cannot bear your worthless assemblies.
[14]Your New Moon feasts and your appointed festivals
I hate with all my being.
They have become a burden to me;
I am weary of bearing them.
[15]When you spread out your hands in prayer,
I hide my eyes from you;
even when you offer many prayers,
I am not listening.
Your hands are full of blood! (NIV)

A similar message was repeated in Amos 5:21-24.
[21]"I hate all your show and pretense—
the hypocrisy of your religious festivals and solemn assemblies.
[22]I will not accept your burnt offerings and grain offerings.
I won't even notice all your choice peace offerings.
[23]Away with your noisy hymns of praise!
I will not listen to the music of your harps.
[24]Instead, I want to see a mighty flood of justice,
an endless river of righteous living.

They were doing what the Law said. They were doing what God TOLD them to do. If they were doing God's good works, why weren't they bringing glory to God? Why was God angry at them?

Too often, many of us live like this. For too long I wondered how many 'right' things I had to do, to be in God's 'good' book. It took me a long time to realize I could do activities (or works) all my life, and never be right with God.

Worshiping God is not about the things we do. Being right with God is not based on our actions. If this were the case, we could earn our way into God's favour. The Bible says this is impossible.

Romans 3:23
For everyone has sinned; we all fall short of God's glorious standard.

Romans 3:27
Can we boast, then, that we have done anything to be accepted by God? No, because our acquittal is not based on obeying the law. It is based on faith.

Let's read Isaiah 1:2-4 and Amos 5:10-14, to understand why God was angry.

Although the people were doing all the right actions, they were also being cruel and unjust to others. To use a modern phrase, they were being "Sunday Christians". On the Sabbath and festival days they did all the right things, but the rest of the time, their actions were exactly the opposite of what God expected.

Their hearts and minds were focused on themselves, on what they wanted to have, what they wanted to do, not on God. Yet they thought they could stay in God's favour, by performing the right actions and ceremonies.

In Isaiah 1:18-20, Amos 5:14-15 and Hosea 6:6, God tells His people what they must do. Although thousands of years have passed, we are no different today, we must still run from sin to God.

Romans 12:1-2 also gives us clear directions for our focus and behaviour.

[1]Therefore, I urge you, brothers and sisters, in view of God's mercy, to offer your bodies as a living sacrifice, holy and pleasing to God—this is your true and proper worship. [2]Do not conform to the pattern of this world, but be transformed by the renewing of your mind. Then you will be able to test and approve what God's will is—his good, pleasing and perfect will. (NIV)

Only when we focus our hearts and minds on God, above all else, can our activities, our actions, our works, be acceptable, because we will not want to do anything that is against His wishes.

When our focus is entirely on God, we realize it is not us who decides what activities, or works, are acceptable to God, it is God alone.

Worship is not about activities. It is all about God.

Learn
Read 1Corinthians 5:9-11, then list the specific actions Paul spoke against.

_____

_____

_____

Think
Based on 1Corinthians 5:9-11 and the passages above, are there any activities in your life right now that God would not be happy with?

_____

_____

Do
It is important to fully understand that God does not condemn you. He loves you deeply, even though He cannot accept your sin. It is our enemy, the devil, who tells us we are too dirty, or too bad, for God. The devil does this to keep us focused on our failures, on our sin, so he can continue to criticize, condemn and control us. But God is always waiting for us. All we are to do is turn and run from our sin, into God's open and loving arms. Which is what 'repent' means. There we WILL receive mercy, love, peace and forgiveness.

Bible reading
Read Romans 3:9-31. This passage tells us that no work, or activity, we do can make us right with God, then tells us what does.

God chat
Talk to God about the things in your life that do not please Him. Ask God to tell you how to run from them into His arms. Then allow Him to show you the mercy, love, peace and forgiveness He has for you.

What Worship Is

Worship is - Submitting to God

Worship is far more than going to church, or shouting hallelujah, or singing a few songs on a Sunday. Worship is a heart attitude first and an action second. Worship is about giving God our all, our heart, soul, mind and body. It's realizing God has given us everything, including our life, and letting Him have full access to everything He has given us, our resources, our skills, our gifts, even our lives.

In the Old Testament, the word worship is found over 100 times. Several Hebrew words are translated into English as worship. Of these words, three are used far more than any others. The most popular, can also mean 'bow down' or 'submit'. The second most common, also means 'serve' and the third also means 'fear'.

The New Testament follows a similar pattern, with the most common Greek word translated as worship also meaning 'kneel before' or 'submit'. The second, also translated as 'serve' and the third, with the meaning of 'fear'.

Therefore, the most common image of worship is like going before a King and kneeling, or bowing, in submission before them.

God's definition of worship incorporates all three meanings into a concept we either don't understand or find disturbing.

Romans 12:1 says, "*Therefore, I urge you, brothers and sisters, in view of God's mercy, to offer your bodies as a living sacrifice, holy and pleasing to God--this is your true and proper worship.*" (NIV)

Worship is not passive. Worship is not a feeling. Worship is not singing songs on Sunday. According to God, worship is death.

Matthew 10:38 & 16:24, Mark 8:34 and Luke 9:23 say serving, and obeying, Jesus means we are to take up our cross. The people of the time knew this meant to die.

This action is also described as being a slave (2Peter 1:1), or a slave to righteousness (Romans 6:18). Technically a slave is dead. Although not physically or mentally dead, they had no say in their life, as their lives belonged to their masters.

In some translations, the word bondservant is used (Romans1:1, Philippians 1:1). The use of bondservant is important, as it represents a slave who has been freed, then chooses to give up their life, their freedom, to commit their lives to become a slave again.

This relates to us in this way. From the moment we are born, we are slaves to sin. We are held captive. We are never given the choice. We are slaves. When we accept that Jesus died to take away all our sin (Jesus as Savior), we are freed from that slavery. We are free to choose. Then, when we accept Jesus as Lord (or Master) we freely choose to become His slave. We become his bond servant (or servant).

In the Old Testament, a bond servant had their ear pierced, as a sign of their choice. Now, we receive the Holy Spirit as that sign. That is why the Holy Spirit only comes to those who choose to serve Jesus.

A bond servant will firstly submit their will and lives to their master, they will then serve, doing what they are told. Lastly, they will 'fear', their master. 'Fear', in this situation, means having a strong understanding that the master has total control over the welfare, and life, of the slave. Slaves are totally reliant on the will and desire of their master.

This is how God wants us to behave toward Him.

It is true we are also described as servants. At the time the Bible was written a servant, or bond servant, was the same as a slave. However, in our modern world, servant has a different meaning. Today, a servant can leave their employer at any time, for any reason. If we see ourselves as servants, we can risk developing a heart attitude that believes serving God is optional, and we can walk away any time we want.

This is one reason many Christians 'walk away' from God or slide back into their old lifestyles (back-slide).

1Corinthians 6 says, *19b You are not your own; 20you were bought at a price. Therefore honor God with your bodies.*

The Greek word translated as 'honour' can also be translated as 'glorify' or 'worship'.

So, where is all this leading and why is it important to worshiping God?

All these definitions mean we give up any rights we have as people when we choose to accept Jesus as our Lord. Worship starts with dying to ourselves and living for God. As Romans 12:1 says, we offer God our lives as a sacrifice, and our living bodies as an offering, which is the only true worship.

In Matthew 10:39 Jesus says, *If you cling to your life, you will lose it; but if you give up your life for me, you will find it.* This same message can be found in Matthew 16:25, Mark 8:35 and Luke 9:24 and 17:33.

The meaning was not lost on those listening, they knew it meant to become a slave, or bond servant, who dies to the life they have lived, to start a new life under their master. In our modern times, we don't see slavery, so phrases and concepts like this, can be missed.

Singer songwriter, Graham Kendrink, is quoted as saying, "Worship has been misunderstood as something that arises from a feeling that 'comes upon you', but it is vital we understand it is rooted in a conscious act of the will, to serve and obey the Lord Jesus Christ."

Although worship is ultimately about expressing our love and adoration for God, it starts with complete submission, goes through the wonderful work of Jesus and ends in an eternity with our loving Lord and Master.

Worship begins with us on our knees saying, "I give everything to you God. My life and all I have is yours."

This is true worship.

Learn
Read Romans chapter 6 and list the times Paul writes about the concept of being a slave.

_____

_____

_____

_____

_____

_____

Think
How is the concept of being a slave to God differ from how you see your current position with God?

_____

_____

_____

Do
Everything God says about us still applies. We are still His children. He still loves us so deeply He works in our lives every day, to bring us closer to Him.

The concept of slavery is important, so we completely understand God must always be in charge. We are to let God be in control, not anyone else, including ourselves. We are to do as God tells us, not vice versa.

Bible reading
Read Romans chapter 8. This chapter tells of the benefits of letting God rule our lives.

God chat
Talk to God about your attitude toward Him and ask for forgiveness of any attitude, that would not please Him.

Give your life to Him and ask Him to direct you, knowing His plans for you are wonderful and are for your benefit not harm.

Then allow Him to respond. This may take some time, especially if we are not used to listening to God. Be patient, He will answer. Maybe not today, nor tomorrow, but He will. God knows a slave, and a child, will wait. Sometimes He reminds us of this fact.

WORSHIP

Part 2 - How We Worship

Worship is a combination of attitude and action. In the previous section we understood that worship is submission to God. Now we will explore how we can express our love toward God. This begins with an attitude that God is everything in our lives.

There are three things God is looking for when we worship Him. Submission, Reverence and Adoration. All heart attitudes.

In Kim Walker-Smith's song, Just Be, she sings about everything else waiting because she is seeking God's face. Further into the song, she sings about wanting nothing more than God, and His presence, because nothing is more important.

Through words like these we are telling God nothing is more important, nothing is more amazing, and nothing is more loved than Him. Nothing.

These words reflect Bible verses, such as these:

Psalm 139:14
I will give thanks to You, for I am fearfully and wonderfully made;
Wonderful are Your works,
And my soul knows it very well. (NASB)

Psalm 37:4-7a
⁴Take delight in the LORD,
and he will give you your heart's desires.
⁵Commit everything you do to the LORD.
Trust him, and he will help you.
⁶He will make your innocence radiate like the dawn,
and the justice of your cause will shine like the noonday sun.
⁷Be still in the presence of the LORD,
and wait patiently for him to act.

Psalm 16:1-2
¹Keep me safe, O God,
for I have come to you for refuge.
²I said to the LORD, "You are my Master!
Every good thing I have comes from you."

It's words like these we need to say to God. But it's not just the words. God sees past any words we say, or actions we perform. He sees our hearts. It's an attitude God is looking for in us.

As well as submitting, we are to show God reverence, acknowledging Him as creator and ruler of the universe. As Elihu did in Job 37:23-24, when he said:

23We cannot imagine the power of the Almighty;
but even though he is just and righteous,
he does not destroy us.
24No wonder people everywhere fear him.
All who are wise show him reverence.

When Job forgot to acknowledge God for who He really is, God reminded him. Take a few minutes and read Job chapters 38 to 42. This passage makes it clear who is in control of this earth and everything in it. (Hint - it's not us.) If we ever start to think we are in control, it is good to read this passage again.

God also wants us to praise Him for all He does for us, especially for His salvation and grace, as the Apostle Paul writes in Romans 3:23-24.

23For everyone has sinned; we all fall short of God's glorious standard. 24Yet God, in his grace, freely makes us right in his sight. He did this through Christ Jesus when he freed us from the penalty for our sins.

A part of this is to express the love we have for Him, because of all He has done for us. Deuteronomy 6:5, Mark 12:30-33 and Luke 10:27, tell us we are to love God with all our heart (our spirit) and soul (our thoughts, emotions and will) and strength (our body).

This may seem contrary to everything we are taught in this world, and sometimes even in our churches but, as slaves, as bond servants, we need to acknowledge God for who He is and allow Him to direct us and teach us.

The world wants to grab our attention. People want us to put them first. We want to put ourselves first. In Matthew 10:37 Jesus makes this point very clearly, when. He says, *"If you love your father or mother more than you love me, you are not worthy of being mine; or if you love your son or daughter more than me, you are not worthy of being mine."*

He is saying, if we make anyone, or anything, more important than God, we are not putting God first, we are not serving God first, we are not worshiping God, we are worshiping them. It may sound hard and harsh, but ultimately God is saying, "If you had to decide between Me and another, who would you choose?" For many of us, this decision is not as easy as it first seems.

This does not mean we cannot care for others. God instructs us to love others, as we love ourselves. So, loving and caring for others is an essential part of the life God wants for us. It comes down to who we love most and who we choose first.

In Matthew 6:33, Jesus confirms this when He says, "*Seek the Kingdom of God above all else, and live righteously, and he will give you everything you need.*"

When we begin to create an attitude in our lives, that shows submission, reverence and love toward God, then our actions reflect our attitude.

Jesus tells us to cut off our hand if it causes us to sin. But our hand can never cause us to sin. Sin comes from a thought pattern, that creates a heart attitude that turns into an action.

Our thoughts centre around what is most important to us. That is why God constantly reminds us to focus on Him far more than anything else.

Learn
How do the words 'Everything else can wait' explain the attitude God wants us to have toward worshiping Him?

_____

_____

_____

_____

Think
If you had to choose between God and someone / something else, would you choose God first? Why?

_____

_____

_____

_Do_

As our thoughts create our heart attitude which drives our behaviour, what thought do you need to address, to create an attitude to aligns with what God requires?

_____

_____

_____

Bible reading

Read Isaiah 40:10-31. This passage tells us about God's power and authority.
Read 1Peter 1:13-25. This passage tells of the benefits of living for God.

God chat

Talk to God about how you can put Him first.

Putting God first does not come naturally, for any of us. We need God's help to do this. So, when you struggle, don't feel you have failed, or allow the devil to condemn you. It is a lifetime's work. The closer we come to God, the more of God's love, peace and joy we want, which leads us to yearning to spend more time with Him.

God made us to yearn for Him. Unfortunately, too many of us fill that need with things other than God. That is why the life God wants for us has Him as the focus.

Worship in Action

Previously we talked about activities, actions and works not being worship. On their own they are not. When our heart attitude is in alignment with God, then any activity can be worship.

In the Jesus Culture version of the song Great Defender, Katie Torwalt sings about praise being her breakthrough, about worship being a form of warfare and about God being our victory.

Through these words, she is telling us God turns worship into actions. Praising God brings breakthrough in our lives. Singing to God brings us triumph. Worshiping God is how our battles are fought. This song begins with God going to fight a battle, before we know, then returning to call it our victory.

This truth is found in passages like Joshua 6:1-16 and 2Chronicles 20:15-24, which describes the victories God gave his people.

Psalm 149 also talks about God giving us victory through our praise and worship of Him.

¹Praise the LORD!
Sing to the LORD a new song.
Sing his praises in the assembly of the faithful.
²O Israel, rejoice in your Maker.
O people of Jerusalem, exult in your King.
³Praise his name with dancing,
accompanied by tambourine and harp.
⁴For the LORD delights in his people;
he crowns the humble with victory.
⁵Let the faithful rejoice that he honors them.
Let them sing for joy as they lie on their beds.
⁶Let the praises of God be in their mouths,
and a sharp sword in their hands—
⁷to execute vengeance on the nations
and punishment on the peoples,
⁸to bind their kings with shackles
and their leaders with iron chains,
⁹to execute the judgment written against them.
This is the glorious privilege of his faithful ones.
Praise the LORD!

Psalm 149 applies to us, when we view it through the truth in Ephesians 6:12, which says, *"For our struggle is not against flesh and blood, but against the rulers, against the powers, against the world forces of this darkness, against the spiritual forces of wickedness in the heavenly places."* (NASB)

45

Then the sharp sword in verse 6 is the Word of God, the Bible, and the people, kings and leaders in verses 7 and 8 are the spiritual forces working for the devil, and the judgement is God's.

Worship is not passive. It is the opposite. In this world, we may not see worship doing anything, but we need to have faith, which means certainty, that when we praise, worship and sing to God, we open ourselves for God to work through us, to defeat those spiritual forces. These are the forces that affect the behaviour of people, the health of people and the eternity (salvation) of people.

The more we do this, the more God can use us. That is why it is vital we have the correct attitude. That is why we spent so much time building our foundation for worship. God cannot effectively use us if our words say one thing and our hearts say another.

Now we understand worship, we can go to church and sing songs directly to God. No longer will they be words we just say, they can be a musical prayer time, where we mean every word. They become worship.

Now when we go to work, or to the store, we can do those everyday activities as if we are doing them with God, as if we are doing them for Him, for He is our constant companion and the reason we do all things. Every activity we do can have an opportunity to do something for God, when we make ourselves available to serve Him, to honour Him and to love Him.

Then when we're alone, we can have a special time with God, that I call the Throne Room experience.

The Throne Room experience
The throne room experience is not a prayer time, nor is it a time to share with others. It is a special time for us to spend with God. Some people can call this the Secret Place, or Closet time.

For this experience, you need time alone. This time can be as little as a few minutes, or it can be hours. You can do it while on a bathroom break, or on a weekend retreat. It is not about location. It is about connecting with God.

The throne room experience can change from day to day. Yet, every time we do it, we get closer to God, we yearn for more of what He teaches us, for more of His presence. Ephesians 3:19 says we can be filled with all the fullness of God. However, when we are bombarded with the things of this world, we can find it hard to focus on God's presence.

This is not an emotion or feeling based experience, although we can become emotional. It is entirely about giving 100% of our focus to God, giving 100% of ourselves to God and giving 100% of our devotion to God.

Here is how we do it.

If we have been living deliberately sinful lives, we need to approach in the way James 4:8-10 describes, as sin cannot be in God's presence and we need to be right with God first.

James 4:8-10

8Come close to God, and God will come close to you. Wash your hands, you sinners; purify your hearts, for your loyalty is divided between God and the world. 9Let there be tears for what you have done. Let there be sorrow and deep grief. Let there be sadness instead of laughter, and gloom instead of joy. 10Humble yourselves before the Lord, and he will lift you up in honor.

When we do this, God lifts us up into His honour, into His glory, into a place we can have relationship with Him.

When we are in relationship with God, we can approach in the ways described below, because we know God has forgiven our sins and we know God wants us close.

Hebrews 4:16

So let us come boldly to the throne of our gracious God. There we will receive his mercy, and we will find grace to help us when we need it most.

Ephesians 3:12

Because of Christ and our faith in him, we can now come boldly and confidently into God's presence.

If it helps, we can imagine we are standing at the entrance to God's throne room, looking through the open doorway. Our Father God is on the throne. Jesus sits on His right. The Holy Spirit is hovering over the whole scene. God calls our name and says, "Come close my child. You are welcome." What would you do?

Realizing, the moment we enter, our sin is gone, our past is gone, our hurts are gone. In God's presence there is no condemnation, there is no guilt, there is only love, joy, peace, patience, kindness and gentleness. What would you do?

Some will fall on their knees and cry. Some will run to lay at his feet. Some will sing. Some will raise their arms and praise God with everything they have. What will you do?

Revelations 4:8-11 and 5:9:14 tell us what the heavenly creatures do in God's presence.

Revelations 4:8-11

8b and day and night they do not cease to say,
"HOLY, HOLY, HOLY is THE LORD GOD, THE ALMIGHTY, WHO WAS AND WHO IS AND WHO IS TO COME."

⁹And when the living creatures give glory and honor and thanks to Him who sits on the throne, to Him who lives forever and ever, ¹⁰the twenty-four elders will fall down before Him who sits on the throne, and will worship Him who lives forever and ever, and will cast their crowns before the throne, saying, ¹¹"Worthy are You, our Lord and our God, to receive glory and honor and power; for You created all things, and because of Your will they existed, and were created." (NASB)

Revelations chapter 5:11-14
¹¹Then I looked, and I heard the voice of many angels around the throne and the living creatures and the elders; and the number of them was myriads of myriads, and thousands of thousands, ¹²saying with a loud voice,
"Worthy is the Lamb that was slain to receive power and riches and wisdom and might and honor and glory and blessing."
¹³And every created thing which is in heaven and on the earth and under the earth and on the sea, and all things in them, I heard saying, "To Him who sits on the throne, and to the Lamb, be blessing and honor and glory and dominion forever and ever."
¹⁴And the four living creatures kept saying, "Amen." And the elders fell down and worshiped. (NASB)

What you do will be different to anyone else. God has made you unique and special. Your heart and mind are different to all others. You may do some, all or none of these things. I know what I often do. I fall on my knees and say, "Father, show me and tell me what YOU want me to do." Then I wait for Him. What will you do?

Think about it. Imagine it. This is not something we will only do in Heaven. When we accept Jesus as Savior and Lord, God comes to live in us. Therefore, we can be in God's presence at any time. This is not a future activity. It is something for now.

What will you do?

Learn
Read Psalms 149 and 150, then list the different ways the psalmist praises and worships God.

_____

_____

_____

_____

_____

Think
How many ways, or activities, can you use to express worship for God?

_____

_____

_____

_____

_____

Do
God doesn't need our worship. He wants us to worship Him, so our hearts grow closer to Him. Considering this, and the list of ways to worship you've written, start worshiping God in ways you may not have done so before.

Bible reading
Read Isaiah 42:1-16. This passage covers many of the areas we have discussed, from our salvation to God's power to how we praise and worship Him.

God chat
Spend time in the Throne Room.
From now on, start every prayer time worshiping God. It will change your prayer time dramatically.

The Next Step

So far, we have come to understand the wonderful news about who God says we are. With this information, we can remove the negative images this world tries to put on us. We can trust God does not lie to us and build on the truth He tells us.

We have also come to understand how and why we truly worship. How our heart attitude is far more important than any actions we may do. We understand how important it is to make God the focus and centre of our lives.

Now we can know worship can happen anytime and anywhere, because God is with us all the time, we may even be finding new ways and opportunities to worship God, because we've learnt that praising and worshiping God is how we fight our battles.

For some of us, these ideas and actions may be new and possibly challenging. If this is the case, I want to assure you God is working in your life. You may not immediately notice the changes, but others will.

When God works in our lives we are always positively, powerfully and permanently changed. This is not a 'one time only' change. It is a day-by-day change. The more we give Him, the more this occurs. The more we seek God, the more He reveals Himself to us. The more He reveals the more we seek. Test this and you will find it is true.

Now we are coming closer to God, we will look at how God works in our lives and within this world. We have read how he created the world and each of us, but God also works in powerful ways that draws our attention to Him.

These ways are called Miracles, or Signs and Wonders.

MIRACLES

Part 1- Everyone Has Seen a Miracle

The life God wants for us includes miracles.

When we talk about miracles, or signs and wonders, we often think of people being brought back from the dead or Jesus walking on water. Yet many of God's miracles are overlooked.

Starting at the Genesis 1:1, we can see many miracles, which I have underlined, that describe God's miracles.

[1]In the beginning God created the heavens and the earth. [2]The earth was formless and empty, and darkness covered the deep waters.

This is the first recorded miracle. How did God create the earth out of nothing? We cannot even imagine how this could be done. Does that mean God can't? Absolutely not, that is why He is God.

I recently read a quote which said, "God does not do miracles contrary to nature, only to our understanding of nature." (Author unknown) Our understanding of nature is limited to our five senses and the ability of our brains to comprehend. Even the most intelligent of us cannot compare to God. In Isaiah 55:9 God says, *"For as the heavens are higher than the earth, So are My ways higher than your ways And My thoughts than your thoughts."* (NASB)

It is wonderful to know God made everything. He is the Creator. As the Creator, He knows and understands the rules of what we might call 'nature', but God calls 'Creation'.

[3]Then God said, "Let there be light," and there was light.
[5]God called the light "day" and the darkness "night."

We can see things because God created light. Without light, there is absolute darkness. Without light there can be no life, for animals rely on plants, which rely on light. The creation of light is a miracle. An act of God, outside our understanding, but well within God's ability and His rules of Creation.

This is not the light from the sun, as the sun had not yet been created. This light is the light John referred to in Revelations 21:23, when describing God's city, *And the city has no need of the sun or of the moon to shine on it, for the glory of God has illumined it, and its lamp is the Lamb.*

[6]Then God said, "Let there be a space between the waters, to separate the waters of the heavens from the waters of the earth."

⁸God called the space "sky."

God's next miraculous work was to create an air gap between the ocean and clouds that now hover in the sky. We live in this air gap. When we look from the oceans to the clouds above, we can know God did something amazing. The fact that we, as humans, can't do it, or imagine how it could be done, does not affect God.

Here is an example. We make a bird house and put it outside. When a bird comes to nest in it, does it matter to us that the bird does not understand how the house was built? No, what matters is, we have made a home for the bird. Even if we tried to explain the construction to the bird, it would not understand, because our abilities are far beyond the birds, as Isaiah says God's ways are above ours. I'm glad I don't have to figure out how God did everything.

⁹Then God said, "Let the waters beneath the sky flow together into one place, so dry ground may appear." And that is what happened.
¹⁰God called the dry ground "land" and the waters "seas."

Then God separated the seas and made land. Although we don't know how this can be done, it is enough to know God does. He created the land on which we live, miraculously, as only He can.

Look around, look at the soil, and the stones. They were made by God. Jesus confirms this truth in Luke 19:37-40.

³⁷As soon as He was approaching, near the descent of the Mount of Olives, the whole crowd of the disciples began to praise God joyfully with a loud voice for all the miracles which they had seen,
³⁸shouting: "BLESSED IS THE KING WHO COMES IN THE NAME OF THE LORD;
Peace in heaven and glory in the highest!"
³⁹Some of the Pharisees in the crowd said to Him, "Teacher, rebuke Your disciples." ⁴⁰But Jesus answered, "I tell you, if these become silent, the stones will cry out!" (NASB)

In this passage Jesus is saying, "the people recognize I am God. If you silence them, the stones will say the same thing, because they know their Creator."

¹¹Then God said, "Let the land sprout with vegetation—every sort of seed-bearing plant, and trees that grow seed-bearing fruit. These seeds will then produce the kinds of plants and trees from which they came." And that is what happened.

God created vegetation. Life. Not only life, but life that can reproduce. It is only in the last 50 years that scientists have really begun to understand the complexity of DNA. Although some cloning attempts have been made, they still have no idea how to create life. Creating life to successfully reproduce seems impossible. Another miracle that is not too hard for our God.

[14]Then God said, "Let lights appear in the sky to separate the day from the night. Let them be signs to mark the seasons, days, and years.
[15]Let these lights in the sky shine down on the earth."
[16]God made two great lights—the larger one to govern the day, and the smaller one to govern the night. He also made the stars.
[17]God set these lights in the sky to light the earth, [18]to govern the day and night, and to separate the light from the darkness.

Then God created the sun, the moon and the stars. In doing so, he created our concept of time, see verse 14. Man may have divided days into hours, but God created day, night and seasons. They don't control God, God controls them. That is why God is outside time. Verses such as Ephesians 1:4-5 confirm this.

Some of us have been confused by verses like 2Peter 3:8, which say, "*But do not let this one fact escape your notice, beloved, that with the Lord one day is like a thousand years, and a thousand years like one day.*" (NASB) This confusion is due to not understanding God is outside time. This verse means, God can have an overall perspective of time, looking at a thousand of our years, as if it was one of our days. He can also have a very detailed, intimate, perspective, where one of our days would seem like it took a thousand years to pass.

That is why, in verse 9, Peter goes on to say, "*The Lord is not slow about His promise, as some count slowness.*" He is saying God knows His plans and does things exactly when it suits Him, which may not match our timeframe.

Other than time, some of us have issues with being able to see the stars, as mentioned in verses 16 and 17. Occasionally I have people say, they can't believe we can see stars that are millions of light years away if the earth has only existed for thousands of years. This uncertainty comes from a lack of understanding that God, who created light, could easily make the star's light exist between distant stars and us, so it would "shine down on the earth". Another miracle we can see every day and every night.

Although it can be very difficult at times, we need to be aware to never limit God to our limited understanding.

[20]Then God said, "Let the waters swarm with fish and other life. Let the skies be filled with birds of every kind."
[22]Then God blessed them, saying, "Be fruitful and multiply. Let the fish fill the seas, and let the birds multiply on the earth.
[24]Then God said, "Let the earth produce every sort of animal, each producing offspring of the same kind—livestock, small animals that scurry along the ground, and wild animals."

Again, God created life, this time in the form of animals, with thinking brains, which plants lack. Once more, He used the earth to make life.

Some scientists say this may be possible, as life's basic building blocks are in the soil. However, man cannot build, from the start, any form of life, especially a complex, thinking, reproducing form. Even if this was possible, we need to remember, it can only be done from the soil already created by God. A miracle? Absolutely. Depending on how we count them, this is at least the seventh miracle. Seven. All of which, we can see every day and night.

26Then God said, "Let us make human beings in our image, to be like us. They will reign over the fish in the sea, the birds in the sky, the livestock, all the wild animals on the earth, and the small animals that scurry along the ground."
27So God created human beings in his own image.
male and female he created them.
28Then God blessed them and said, "Be fruitful and multiply. Fill the earth and govern it.

Then God made us. Man and woman made like God. That makes us different to everything created before. We are made up of three parts, as God is three parts. Body, soul (our thoughts, emotions and will) and spirit. This is confirmed in Deuteronomy 6:5, Mark 12:30-33 and Luke 10:27, that tell us we are to love God with all our heart (our spirit) and soul and strength (our body).

29Then God said, "Look! I have given you every seed-bearing plant throughout the earth and all the fruit trees for your food. 30And I have given every green plant as food for all the wild animals, the birds in the sky, and the small animals that scurry along the ground—everything that has life."

Finally, not finally for miracles, but finally for Genesis chapter 1, we get to verses 29 and 30, which are also very special.

Atheistic scientists often claim Genesis is a fictitious record of creation, written to suit a religion. However, the entire creation order is completely contrary to any concept a person would create. If we look at the order of creation, we see light is made before the sun, the thing we believe makes light. Vegetation is created before the sun, and plants cannot live without the sun. God knows the light He makes sustains life. The earth is made before light, yet atheistic science says the opposite.

Even verses 29 and 30 contain a contradiction for many scientists. No person seeing what man and animals eat, even in the time of Moses, would have written that God designed all living creatures to only eat green plants. Truths, such as these, can only come from the one who made it happen. God.

God created a way for all animals and man to eat, so no life would be lost, so nothing would be killed. This is His version of survival. It is far from the version that says, "Survival of the fittest." It is far from the version of life existing on the earth now. This perfect order, lost when sin entered the world, will be reinstated in the eternity of Heaven.

Verse 31 gives God's perspective of His Creation. *Then God looked over all he had made, and he saw that it was very good!* (NIV)

God created everything we see, starting with this earth and ending with us, and it was good in His eyes. If we still have any uncertainty, please read Job chapter 38.

Learn
Write your own version of the miracles listed in Genesis chapter 1.

_____

_____

_____

_____

_____

_____

Think
Of all God's creative works, why did He create people last? The answer is in Genesis 1:26-28.

_____

_____

_____

Do
Spend some time looking at God's miracles. See them for what they are: a wonderful creation, living and full, made for the benefit of those he loves deeply - us.

Bible reading
Read Isaiah 65:17-25. This passage is about a new world God will create for His people. A world that does not yet exist. A place we call Heaven.

God chat
Spend time thanking God for the miracles he has performed, remembering to start our prayer time with worship and praise.

God's creative works are all miracles. They cannot be explained, through our knowledge, reasoning or understanding. That does not mean they are impossible for God. What it means is God's miraculous work is around us every moment of every day, and we need to be looking for His hand at work.

When we believe God does miracles, we look for them. When we look for them, we see them. When we see them, we expect them. When we expect them, our faith increases dramatically.

Sometimes, we can see a miracle, but not recognize it, even when it happens to us. There are two miracles, too often missed, which have happened to most of us. I believe these miracles are the two of the greatest miracles.

Two of The Greatest Miracles

If we have accepted Jesus as our Savior and Lord, we have seen two miracles, that happened at the same time.

The first of these miracles is that we are Born Again. Being born again is a wonderful miracle of God. Yes, it did not involve a public display or angels singing (for most of us anyway), but it was a miracle.

If we have seen others give their lives to Jesus, we have seen this miracle.

The second miracle (in order listed, not importance), is when the Holy Spirit comes into us. God Himself comes to live in us. The Creator of the universe chooses to be with us, every second of the day. Giving us full and unlimited access to Him. Always.

Unlike the people of the Old Testament, we no longer need to go through a priest to access God. God has come to us, to share in our lives, so He can always be available to help us.

These are the greatest miracles and miracles He wanted everyone to have. These miracles are a wonderful expression of God's love for us. He loves us so much. He wants to be with us now and for eternity. He gave His Son, Jesus, so we could experience these miracles.

Just before Jesus departed this world, to be with the Father, he gave the Disciples their most important task, which is commonly called the Great Commission. This task is recorded at the end of the gospels of Matthew and Mark.

Matthew 28:18-20
18Jesus came and told his disciples, "I have been given all authority in heaven and on earth. 19Therefore, go and make disciples of all the nations, baptizing them in the name of the Father and the Son and the Holy Spirit. 20Teach these new disciples to obey all the commands I have given you. And be sure of this: I am with you always, even to the end of the age."

Mark 16:15-18.
15And then he told them, "Go into all the world and preach the Good News to everyone. 16Anyone who believes and is baptized will be saved. But anyone who refuses to believe will be condemned. 17These miraculous signs will accompany those who believe: They will cast out demons in my name, and they will speak in new languages. 18They will be able to handle snakes with safety, and if they drink anything poisonous, it won't hurt them. They will be able to place their hands on the sick, and they will be healed."

In the book of John, Jesus also talks about this work we will do.

John 14:12 says,

[12]"I tell you the truth, anyone who believes in me will do the same works I have done, and even greater works, because I am going to be with the Father.

In the last passage, Jesus is telling the Disciples (which is what we are) that they will do greater things than He did, if they believe in Him. What is the main thing Jesus was saying they will do?

It's not healing the sick, nor making the blind see. It's not even raising people from the dead.

The answer is in the first two passages. It is making disciples, which is bringing people into relationship with the Father, and doing it so the Father would be glorified.

Why is that a greater work?

It is a greater work because it is the only permanent work. Although healing is wonderful, it only lasts while our current body is alive. We don't need healing in Heaven. Calming storms or multiplying food, although amazing, only apply while this world exists. Signs and wonders are only temporary, as they are not required in Heaven.

Having someone born again into the family of God ensures an eternity in Heaven. An eternity in God's presence, free of pain and suffering. Having someone receive the Holy Spirit ensures them eternal access to God. That's the greatest work they did and that's the greatest work we can do. These are miracles we all can be involved in.

Learn
Write the requirements Jesus gives in the passages above.

_____

_____

_____

Now, from the passage in Mark, list the signs that will be shown by believers.

_____

_____

_____

_____

Think

Do you notice that signs and wonders are a part of the process, but not the major aim.

Why is it important for us to tell the Good News about Jesus before miracles?

_____

_____

_____

_____

_____

Do
Go back to Identity part 2 and reread the section about the Good News.

Bible reading
Read Isaiah chapter 55. This chapter talks about the Good News. When we come to God and choose Jesus as Savior and Lord, God works the greatest miracles in our lives.

God chat
If you have chosen Jesus as Savior and Lord, thank God for working these miracles in your life and ask Him to work these miracles in the lives of people you know, who have not accepted Jesus as Savior and Lord.

If you have not yet chosen Jesus as Savior and Lord, talk to God about this. Now is an opportunity to make that decision, knowing God will work these miracles in your life.

You could say something like this,

Father God, I know you love me.
I'm sorry for doing the things I want, instead of what you want.
There is nothing I can do, to be right in your eyes except, believe Jesus died to take away my sins and give my life for Jesus to be my Lord.
So, I do that right now. Come and make me new.

If you have said a prayer like this, you can have faith (which means certainty) that you have received the greatest miracles. You are Born Again. The Holy Spirit has come to live in you, and you have begun the life God wants for us.

MIRACLES

Part 2 - The Purpose of Miracles

There are millions, of people outside the walls of our church buildings, who yearn for more than the world can offer. People who are desperately hurting and only God has what they need. The miracle of being Born Again. A miracle happening every day on every continent (even Antarctica when the Gospel is shared).

This does not mean other miracles are not important. God still uses miracles. He uses them for one main reason. To show people His power and love, so people's eyes are drawn to Him, not us. That is why everything we do, even performing miracles, is to glorify God.

Before we continue to discuss miracles, I feel it is important to confirm we cannot do miracles. As humans we have no power to perform any miracle. It is never a person doing a miracle.

For many of us, the idea of miracles happening is strange. Too often, due to a lack of experience, we can believe God no longer does miracles. We can even think, "No one I know has ever seen a miracle happen, so obviously they don't happen anymore." However, to deny miracles is to assume God has, somehow, changed.

From Genesis 1:1 the Bible has many references to God working miracles, and there are many people and ministries with recorded miracles. This is not limited to the charismatic style churches. To be called a 'Saint' in the Catholic Church, one of the requirements is the performance of more than one miracle.

As we saw in the last section, God obeys His rules when working miracles. However, the greatest miracles happen when people accept Jesus. Let's celebrate that.

While we are celebrating the miracle of God's new life, it is important to understand although God can, and will, do miracles as He wishes, His miracles always direct people to Him. The priority is to have people give their lives to Jesus. As stated in Mark 16:15-18, the Gospel (Good News) is to be shared and miracles, signs and wonders will follow. The passage in Mark is not the only example of this.

In the following passages, see if you can identify the miracle and where the Gospel is shared.

Acts 2:42-43

42They devoted themselves to the apostles' teaching and to fellowship, to the breaking of bread and to prayer. 43Everyone was filled with awe at the many wonders and signs performed by the apostles. (NIV)

Acts 3:6-8
6Then Peter said, "Silver or gold I do not have, but what I do have I give you. In the name of Jesus Christ of Nazareth, walk." 7Taking him by the right hand, he helped him up, and instantly the man's feet and ankles became strong. 8He jumped to his feet and began to walk. Then he went with them into the temple courts, walking and jumping, and praising God. (NIV)

Acts 5:14-16
14Nevertheless, more and more men and women believed in the Lord and were added to their number. 15As a result, people brought the sick into the streets and laid them on beds and mats so that at least Peter's shadow might fall on some of them as he passed by. 16Crowds gathered also from the towns around Jerusalem, bringing their sick and those tormented by impure spirits, and all of them were healed. (NIV)

Acts 6:7-8
7So the word of God spread. The number of disciples in Jerusalem increased rapidly, and a large number of priests became obedient to the faith. 8Now Stephen, a man full of God's grace and power, performed great wonders and signs among the people. (NIV)

Acts 9:32-35
32As Peter traveled about the country, he went to visit the Lord's people who lived in Lydda. 33There he found a man named Aeneas, who was paralyzed and had been bedridden for eight years. 34"Aeneas," Peter said to him, "Jesus Christ heals you. Get up and roll up your mat." Immediately Aeneas got up. 35All those who lived in Lydda and Sharon saw him and turned to the Lord. (NIV)

Acts 9:40-43
40Peter sent them all out of the room; then he got down on his knees and prayed. Turning toward the dead woman, he said, "Tabitha, get up." She opened her eyes, and seeing Peter she sat up. 41He took her by the hand and helped her to her feet. Then he called for the believers, especially the widows, and presented her to them alive. 42This became known all over Joppa, and many people believed in the Lord. 43Peter stayed in Joppa for some time with a tanner named Simon. (NIV)

Acts 19:9b-12
9b He took the disciples with him and had discussions daily in the lecture hall of Tyrannus. 10This went on for two years, so that all the Jews and Greeks who lived in the province of Asia heard the word of the Lord.

[11]God did extraordinary miracles through Paul, [12]so that even handkerchiefs and aprons that had touched him were taken to the sick, and their illnesses were cured and the evil spirits left them. (NIV)

Hebrew 2:3-4
[3]how shall we escape if we ignore so great a salvation? This salvation, which was first announced by the Lord, was confirmed to us by those who heard him. [4]God also testified to it by signs, wonders and various miracles, and by gifts of the Holy Spirit distributed according to his will. (NIV)

As you have seen in these, and many more verses, God's priority is not miracles, it is salvation. It is creating sons and daughters to live in His kingdom.

As much as miracles are amazing and awe inspiring, we must never make them our focus. Equally, we must never deny, nor run from them. We are to allow God to work, as only He can, while we are doing the work of making Disciples.

This is the point of Jesus' statement in Matthew 11:20-24.

[20]Then Jesus began to denounce the towns where he had done so many of his miracles, because they hadn't repented of their sins and turned to God. [21]"What sorrow awaits you, Korazin and Bethsaida! For if the miracles I did in you had been done in wicked Tyre and Sidon, their people would have repented of their sins long ago, clothing themselves in burlap and throwing ashes on their heads to show their remorse. [22]I tell you, Tyre and Sidon will be better off on judgment day than you.
[23]"And you people of Capernaum, will you be honored in heaven? No, you will go down to the place of the dead. For if the miracles I did for you had been done in wicked Sodom, it would still be here today. [24]I tell you, even Sodom will be better off on judgment day than you.".

Jesus was aware of the Jewish teaching and culture, which expected God to show up and continually save and restore them, through His miraculous works. The Jews could not, or would not, understand how God's miracles were not the result to be desired. They were signs that showed God was real and active. Signs that should have prompted their hearts to repent, to turn to their miracle working God. Instead, they continued to live their sinful lives and demanded more miracles.

That is why the life God wants for us is about focusing on Him and the greater work He has for us. The bonus is being amazed when He steps in to do something extra.

Whether we live in Asia, Africa and South America, where miracles, like healing and casting out demons happens regularly, or North America, Europe and Australia, where they are less regular, we need to understand miracles happen every day.

Yes, miracles are for today, they are happening daily, even if we do not hear about them. But our aim must be making disciples, by sharing the Good News. If, during this, God wants to show up and work another miracle, then we should celebrate it, not because the miracle happened, but because God has moved in a wonderful way.

Learn
Read Hebrews chapter 11 and write the miracles God did because of their faith.

_____

_____

_____

_____

Think
If God honours faith in Him and obedience to Him, what can you do to allow God to honour your faith? It may help to check your responses in the section on Worship.

_____

_____

_____

Do
Make a commitment to carry out some, or all, of the actions you wrote to show your faith. It may be best to try one thing at a time, so you don't become discouraged. Remember, continuing a walk with God can be a discipline we find difficult. God know this and never expects us to be perfect the first time. He never expects us to be perfect. Perfection is a man-made expectation.

Bible reading
Read 1Corinthians 1:18-2:16. This passage talks about the wisdom of God being greater than the wisdom of man.

God chat
Talk to God about ways we can serve Him, remembering our faith is shown through our works, and our works are the things God wants us to do, not what we (or others) think we should do.

The life God wants for us is one where we are doing His work and expecting Him to show up in a miraculous way. Whether God does, or does not, is up to

Him, not us. We are never to feel we are superior because He has done a miracle, or inferior because He has not. We are only to feel loved and accepted because He has work for us to do.

How Do We React to Miracles?

Opinions on miracles vary greatly across Christianity. Other than those Christians who try to deny God is Creator (yes, they are real), Christians rarely deny God can do miracles. The vast difference in opinion is whether miracles like healing, casting out demons and changing weather can happen now.

Before we continue into a discussion on these types of miracles, it is important to understand miracles fall into two general groups. These are signs and wonders.

'Wonders' include miracles like Creation in Genesis chapter 1, manna from Heaven in Exodus chapter 16, the walls of Jericho falling in Joshua chapter 6, instant healing, raising from the dead and calming storms in the New Testament.

'Signs' include miracles like prophesy, words of knowledge (knowing something about someone that we cannot know) and visions.

Throughout the Bible God uses signs and wonders in two main ways. Firstly, to direct our focus to Him and His great powers, and secondly, to direct us to the work He is doing through someone.

Either way, miracles are to bring glory to God. In John 14:12-13, Jesus speaks about this.

[12] "I tell you the truth, anyone who believes in me will do the same works I have done, and even greater works, because I am going to be with the Father. [13] You can ask for anything in my name, and I will do it, so that the Son can bring glory to the Father.

In this passage, Jesus tells us, if we believe in Him, we will do greater works and anything we ask for will be given to us.

I would like to correct some misunderstandings we can have from these verses.

Firstly (and this must happen first), 'believing in Him' is far more than believing Jesus lived, or even that Jesus died for us. Those who 'believe' are only those who have made Jesus their Master. Remember the attitude we discussed in Worship. We are slaves to God. 100% committed to doing exactly what God wants.

Secondly, 'asking for anything' depends on 'believing'. When we are 100% committed to God, the only things we will ask for are things that will allow us to do the same as Jesus, or greater work. I'm sorry to inform you, but it is incredibly unlikely to include a new BMW or a million dollars.

Lastly, it is to bring glory to the Father. It MUST glorify God only. Period.

So, when we hear of claims, from ministries, or individuals, that people are being healed or freed from demons, the only question we should ask is, "Is it glorifying God alone?"

We can argue all day about what is, and is not, a miracle. However, we must never deny God can, and will, do miracles when and how He chooses, through whomever He chooses. Even if that person does not comply with our version of Christianity.

I know that may sound harsh, but God will never fit into any theological 'box' we may have designed for Him. He is God. He makes the rules. If He wants to miraculously heal atheists, or give visions of hell to Muslims, (He has done both) what right do we have to say He shouldn't.

When I was a new Christian, about a year after accepting Jesus, a few of us stood outside a friend's house, watching a storm approach. As the clouds grew more threatening, we could see the centre of the clouds were coloured green which, in my part of the world, means hail.

We had recently heard of people who prayed against storms and saw them change direction. So, we prayed for the storm to go back where it came from. Then we stood in faith. Within a few minutes the storm stopped approaching and went back in the direction it had come.

Can I prove this was a miracle? No. Do I believe it was? Yes. Did we glorify God for what He did? Absolutely. We reacted to a miracle in the way God wants.

Since that time, I have witnessed many instances of signs and wonders. Can I prove, beyond any doubt, any of them were miracles? (Which is what some of us demand) No. Do I believe they were? Yes. Did each instance cause people to glorify God? Absolutely.

Please remember, none of us can perform miracles. We do not have that power and never will, but God does. All we are to do is react to miracles by glorifying Him and Him alone.

When we believe God does miracles, we look for them. When we look for them, we see them. When we see them, we expect them. When we expect them, our faith increases.

Many of us may never see a healing, a demon cast out, or a storm turned away. This does not mean it is not God's plan for them to happen, as stated by these three passages.

1Corinthians 12:27-31
[27]Now you are Christ's body, and individually members of it. [28]And God has appointed in the church, first apostles, second prophets, third teachers, then miracles, then gifts of healings, helps, administrations, various kinds of tongues.

29All are not apostles, are they? All are not prophets, are they? All are not teachers, are they? All are not workers of miracles, are they? 30All do not have gifts of healings, do they? All do not speak with tongues, do they? All do not interpret, do they? 31But earnestly desire the greater gifts. (NASB)

Mark 16:15-18
15And He said to them, "Go into all the world and preach the gospel to all creation. 16"He who has believed and has been baptized shall be saved; but he who has disbelieved shall be condemned. 17"These signs will accompany those who have believed: in My name they will cast out demons, they will speak with new tongues; 18they will pick up serpents, and if they drink any deadly poison, it will not hurt them; they will lay hands on the sick, and they will recover." (NASB)

Hebrews 2:3b-4
3b This salvation, which was first announced by the Lord, was confirmed to us by those who heard him. 4God also testified to it by signs, wonders and various miracles, and by gifts of the Holy Spirit distributed according to his will. (NIV)

1Corinthians 12:28 says, *And God has appointed in the <u>church</u>*. It says gifts, including miracles and healing are appointed to the church. Which is us.

Mark 16:17 says, *These signs will accompany <u>those who have believed</u>*. This verse tells us casting out demons and healing are signs that accompany those who believe. Which is us.

Hebrews 2:4 tells us that miracles will be *distributed <u>according to his will</u>*. That is God's will, not ours. We can want them with all our heart, and they may not happen. We can deny them until we die, and they will still happen. This is because God does them according to His will, not ours.

Knowing this, we can never make miracles our focus, or we risk desiring the gift, not the giver, we risk believing God is not working, unless we see a miracle. Even though we may desire, and expect a miracle, our body, soul and spirit must always be focus on God, regardless of the outcome.

Learn
From the three passages above, write the most important activity / gifts. Hint: it's not miracles.

If you're struggling with this, look at the previous section on The Greatest Miracle.

_____

_____

_____

Think
Why do you think this activity is more important?

_____

_____

_____

Do
Think about how you consider miracles. Does this align with how God wants miracles to be understood?

Bible reading
Read 1Corinthians chapter 12 and take time to think about God's spiritual gifts.

God chat
Talk to God about spiritual gifts and ask Him to show you the gift, or gifts, He has for you. Also ask for His guidance and wisdom on how to use it.

The Next Step

So far, we have discovered, the life God wants for us is far more about what God wants, than we do.

Firstly, He wants us to believe His version of our Identity. Which is who and what He says we are, rather than the lies the world, and our enemy, wants us to believe.

When we think about all the wonderful things God says about us, it always has a positive result. It always makes us realize how much God loves us and how special we are to Him. Knowing this makes us want to love Him in return.

Secondly, God wants us to understand true worship is not about us, or what we do. Worship is always about submitting ourselves, body, mind and spirit, to Him as our Lord, then praising and glorifying Him for all He has done.

 By freeing us from slavery to sin, under the rule of our enemy, God has allowed us to freely choose Him. This choice is to give ourselves completely, as a bondservant, a slave. When we do this, He gives us the privilege of being a son, with an eternal inheritance in Heaven. None of which we deserve.

Thirdly, He wants us to know He has performed miracles since the creation of this world and continues to do miracles when, how and through whom He chooses.

The greatest miracles of all involve us personally. We are Born Again, and God's Holy Spirit comes to live in us. But God doesn't leave it at that. He wants us to expect, look for and find His miraculous work, then glorify Him when we see it.

Finally, He also wants us to tell others all we have learnt about Him. This is our most important work and is nowhere near as hard as many of us believe it to be. All we must do is follow the simple order He gives us.

Let's find out.

SHARING

Part 1 - Why We Share

People submitting to Jesus and coming into God's family, doesn't 'just happen'. Regardless of where, or when, people become Christians, it always involves God working through people like us.

Although there are many testimonies of people who received a vision, dream or spoken word directly from God, in almost every circumstance a person has previously come into their lives and shared the Good News.

God wants everyone to know Him and He wants us to be a part of the process. That is why Jesus gave the Disciples their most important task, the Great Commission. This task is recorded in Matthew 28:18-20 and Mark 16:15-18.

Like all tasks God gives us, sharing about God to others, which is how we make Disciples, should never be done purely as a task we must perform. Remember what we discussed in the section on Worship.

As always, God tells us why He wants us to share and the attitude we should have when sharing.

In Matthew 22:37 Jesus says the greatest commandment is, *You must love the Lord your God with all your heart, all your soul, and all your mind.*
Then in verse 39 he adds, *A second is equally important: Love your neighbour as yourself.*

Verse 39 is the key. Love others (our neighbours) <u>as we love ourselves</u>.

There are lots of ways we can love others. There are lots of things we can do to show God cares. So, instead of starting with how we can love others, we need to understand the best way we love ourselves.

The answer is in verse 37. <u>You must love the Lord your God with all your heart, all your soul, and all your mind</u>.

We love ourselves best by loving God first.

When we love God first, He loves us and provides for us in return. When we give God every part of our lives, by accepting Jesus as Savior and Lord, He gives us a new life. A life directed by Him that is for our gain, not our harm. A life that has a guaranteed inheritance in Heaven, with Him. We can provide food, shelter and care (and we should) but nothing is better than loving God first and above all else.

Therefore, the best way to love others is to help them to do the same. Sharing with others is about showing others God loves them deeply and doing it in such a way they want what we have.

From my discussions with Christians, over thirty years, I have found many of us believe caring for others is a far higher priority than sharing about God. Yet, in Luke 9:59-62, Jesus tells us something different.

Luke 9:59-62
⁵⁹He said to another person, "Come, follow me."
The man agreed, but he said, "Lord, first let me return home and bury my father."
⁶⁰But Jesus told him, "Let the spiritually dead bury their own dead! Your duty is to go and preach about the Kingdom of God."
⁶¹Another said, "Yes, Lord, I will follow you, but first let me say good-bye to my family."
⁶²But Jesus told him, "Anyone who puts a hand to the plow and then looks back is not fit for the Kingdom of God.

In these verses Jesus is saying our priority is to serve Him, not to do the things the world expects us to do. When we first read these verses, they seem harsh, and nothing like the loving Jesus we are taught about, yet they align with Matthew 10:34-39.

³⁴"Do not suppose that I have come to bring peace to the earth. I did not come to bring peace, but a sword. ³⁵For I have come to turn "☐ 'a man against his father, a daughter against her mother,
a daughter-in-law against her mother-in-law— ³⁶a man's enemies will be the members of his own household.'
³⁷"Anyone who loves their father or mother more than me is not worthy of me; anyone who loves their son or daughter more than me is not worthy of me. ³⁸Whoever does not take up their cross and follow me is not worthy of me. ³⁹Whoever finds their life will lose it, and whoever loses their life for my sake will find it. (NIV)

Over the years the image of Jesus has been softened until, for many of us, Jesus is merely a nice man, who said nice things and did nice things, to make people feel nice. So, that is the version of Jesus we try to copy.

As much as this is a sweet, people pleasing image, it is far from the Jesus of the Bible. As Jesus says in Matthew 10:34, "*Do not suppose that I have come to bring peace to the earth. I did not come to bring peace, but a sword*" (NIV). Yes, they are fighting words. Jesus' first aim was to build His Father's kingdom and destroy the kingdom of the enemy in the process. In the two passages above, He clearly states, the priority of His followers is to love Him more than anything else, and to spread the Gospel before anything else. As His servants, it includes us.

Yes, the Bible tells us to care for the widows, the orphans and the poor, but when we read those passages in context (in relation to the verse around them), we almost always find it is those within the church, meaning other believers, we are to care for. In the instances when we care for those outside the church, it is to show and share God's love for them. Providing for the poor, the sick and the hurting is not our main aim, making Disciples is.

Let me explain. Imagine we gave food to the poor, or nursed the sick, or comforted the hurting, all our lives, but never shared the Gospel. When those people died, they all went to hell. What have we achieved? Have those people gained anything from all our effort? Have we truly done what God wants us to do? If all we do is provide things, have we really given anything?

Jesus confirms this when, in Matthew 16:26, He says, *And what do you benefit if you gain the whole world but lose your own soul? 1 Is anything worth more than your soul?*

We can gain, or give others, the whole world, but if their soul is lost, what have they gained? From God's perspective, the answer is "nothing". So, bringing others into a relationship with God, so they love Him above all else, must always be our first objective.

When we read the works and words of Jesus, it is important to remember most of His time was spent sharing with the Jews, who were God's people. See Matthew 10:5-8. The modern equivalent is preaching within the church. There were rare instances when He went to people who were not Jews. One is the story of the Samaritan woman in John chapter 4.

Learn
Read John 4:1-42 and write down Jesus' priority in His exchange with this woman.

Think
Why would Jesus' priority be to bring people to God first.

Do
Think about how important sharing God's Good News is to you. Write a priority list for activities in your life.

Bible reading
Read Matthew chapter 10.

God chat
Talk to God about His priorities for your life and ask Him to show you how to make a His work the priority.

SHARING

Part 2 - How Do I Share?

Now we understand the importance of sharing God's love with others, I want to address another term commonly used for this activity. Outreach.

I do not use the term 'Outreach', as it can create images of being uncomfortable talking to strangers. God's plan never makes us feel uncomfortable sharing about Him.

I discovered this the hard way.

Early in my Christian walk, I was involved in an outreach and discipleship program through the church I was attending. The Pastor and church leaders had a desire to tell others the Good News, exactly as God desires for us.

After a short training course, I was armed with my 'Discipleship Kit', including the 'Roman Road' (a list of verses from the book of Romans to help lead non-Christians to Christ), a pre-scripted 'Sinner's Prayer' and a list of Bible studies to help new Christians to grow.

There is nothing wrong with any of the tools, all can be used effectively when sharing. There was nothing wrong with the churches desire or actions. The problem was I had no idea what I was sharing.

The training gave me ideas on how to share and the importance of repenting from a life of sin, both of which are important. However, I had no idea how deeply God loved me, my 'Identity', or what true 'Worship' was, or the wonders of a miracle working God.

Worst of all, I believed I was totally responsible for bringing a person to Christ, making them a fully functional Disciple and teaching them to repeat the process.

Result - failure.

Although my friend, who I chose to share with, said he accepted Jesus, he never attended church, didn't read the Bible I bought him and, after a few weeks, started avoiding me.

There were a few success stories, but from other members of the church. For years afterward I avoided anything to do with Outreach. I felt demoralized that I was not good enough to make a Disciple and believed the process was too hard. Failure.

Although my Church's intentions were wonderful, unless we understand who God is, who He says we are and how we are to share His message, many of us can feel the same way.

Most of us believe sharing starts with speaking to non-Christians, about God's Good News and love. Yet, that is the last step. Much is to happen beforehand. To expect us, with only a few weeks of training, to make Disciples, is like expecting a sports beginner to compete at the Olympics - and win. As I experienced, the result is rarely positive.

Steps to Sharing
To start with, it is vital to understand, making Disciples is NEVER a task we do alone. It is ALWAYS achieved with the help of other Christians, for we are to work together as one body.

I know this process can feel terrifying, this is often because we have not been given a simple, step by step, process, that builds our ability to share. There are five steps, which build on each other, allowing us to do this.

The basis for these steps is given in Acts 1:8
But you will receive power when the Holy Spirit comes upon you. And you will be my witnesses, telling people about me everywhere—in Jerusalem, throughout Judea, in Samaria, and to the ends of the earth."

Step 1 - When the Holy Spirit comes on you
Luke 24:52-53 tells of the time just after Jesus rose to Heaven.
52So they worshiped him and then returned to Jerusalem filled with great joy. 53And they spent all of their time in the Temple, praising God.

Between the time Jesus left them, and the arrival of the Holy Spirit (Acts chapter 2), the Disciples were focused on worshiping God until, the Holy Spirit came and worked through them.

Like the Disciples, sharing starts with us. It starts by having time with God and allowing Him to share His Good News and love with us. This can start with something as easy as setting time aside to be with God, as we learnt earlier in this book. The first three sections of this book are aimed at building our time with and knowledge of God.

This time will vary for each of us until, like the Disciples, the Holy Spirit works through us. This is different to receiving the Holy Spirit when we accept Jesus. Let me explain.

When we are Born Again the Holy Spirit comes into us, which is God living in us. This is a once only action.

However, the role of the Holy Spirit within us is not passive. The Holy Spirit is God, and God wants to work through us to reach others. This is something that happens as many times as God desires, and we allow.

I know we have no power to stop God however, because God loves us so much, He will not force Himself on us and He will not work through us, if we don't want Him to, or we resist.

Therefore, the more we worship and give ourselves completely to God, the more the Holy Spirit is willing to work through us, until He does wonderful things. As He did for Peter in Acts chapters 2 to 4, He can give us courage and speak through us, to tell others about God. He can also heal, give prophesy and anything else God decides, if we make ourselves available.

While we are establishing a time with God, we also need to learn more about the wonderful things of God. This can be done by spending time with other Christians, by attending Church, small group (home group) meetings through your church and bible studies.

Learning about God is not a one-off activity, it is an ongoing process and will continue throughout our lives, that is the foundation for all other steps.

Once we have started this process, we are ready for the next step.

Step 2 - Telling people In Jerusalem.
Although sharing starts within us, it needs to quickly move to the next step. The longer we hesitate, the more we believe we need to know more before we can share. This is a misunderstanding, based on the idea the only people we will share with are non-Christians.

The second step is telling people in Jerusalem. These people are your close Christian friends and family members who are Christians.

These are the people you are very comfortable with. Comfortable enough to make mistakes. Comfortable enough to have relaxed conversations about God. It is these conversations where we learn to express our thoughts, where we can be challenged to learn more and seek God more and where we can challenge others to do the same.

By sharing with those we are very close to and very comfortable with, we gain confidence with our ability to share. If we were to have these first discussions with non-Christians and we experienced negativity or opposition, which does happen, it is quite possible we could be discouraged from having a similar conversation with others.

There will be some of us who do not yet have close Christian friends. In these instances, we could try to book time with our Pastor, maybe an hour every two to four weeks, so we have a set time. Otherwise attending our churches small groups can help build those connections.

The best, and by far the easiest, way is 'live it don't preach it'. Let me explain.

Firstly, we share about God's love. This is more than telling them what we learnt in the section on Identity. As we believe God deeply loves everyone, we will allow God to show His love through us. The saying "Actions speak louder than words" always applies. Often, the act of loving people, who feel they don't deserve it, prompts them to ask us why we love. Allowing us to share more about God. It is amazing how many people, including Christians, are unaware how deeply God loves them.

Secondly, we share about worshipping God. Again, this is best done through our actions first. When we submit to God and give all to Him, others will notice. When we thank and praise God, regardless of the situation, others will notice. Then they will ask, and we can share about what we have learnt in the section on Worship.

Lastly, we show others we believe in a miracle working God. We do this best by praying for them. Not secretly, although I encourage us to do this as well, but by asking if we can pray for them, then praying with them. Pray for a good result, pray for healing, pray for whatever they need, always expecting a positive outcome.

I know many of us are asking, "What if I pray and nothing happens?"

If we pray and nothing changes, that does not mean God is not working. Remember, God's plans are higher and better than ours, which means there are times our prayers are not answered the way we expect or want. That should never mean we stop believing in a miracle working God.

The question we should ask is, "What if I pray and something does happen?"

How would that change us and the person we are praying for? I know the answer. I've seen it happen. It is a wonderful and positive change.

It is this same pattern of action, discussion and prayer we are to repeat, when we are sharing with people in Judea, Samaria and the rest of the world.

For most of us it is best we share with those in Jerusalem for two to six months. Any shorter and we may be too uncomfortable and may struggle to continue. Any longer and, once more, we risk believing we need more to be able to proceed.

Yes, we will be nervous every time we move to the next step. That is good. It stops us relying on our wisdom and abilities and makes us rely on God, which is what we are supposed to do.

Step 3 - Telling People in Judea

Judea is other Christians in our church. These are people we may have met one time or twenty times. An ideal time for sharing with people in Judea is directly after the Church service, during the time for coffee, or tea. This is ideal as it allows for a continued discussion on the message preached or we could share about 'Identity', 'Worship' and 'Miracles' that we began with those close to us.

Unfortunately, I have attended too many church services where God is rarely discussed during the time afterwards. If this is your experience, it may be a little difficult to start a conversation, but well worth trying.

Another great time for these discussions is at small groups or bible studies, as they allow us to talk with people we may rarely have conversations with.

As with the step 2, we are discussing with people who know about God, even if they do not know God personally (there is a difference). This means we still can make mistakes and improve our knowledge. However, others in our churches may not be as polite as our close friends and family. We may also find, even in our own churches, a range of opinions on many aspects of God.

These different opinions will force us to go back to the Bible, to check the accuracy of our belief. If we are certain others in our church have an incorrect opinion, please do not bluntly tell them they are wrong. This can cause offence, especially as long held opinions can be difficult to change.

Instead, I suggest we meet privately, or quietly, and explain how and why we believe as we do, then allow them to check it out for themselves. Sometimes, they will take a long time to agree and sometimes they never will.

Regardless of the outcome, realize not everyone agrees with God, and He's 100% right all the time, so people will not agree with us, even if we are right. All we are to do is love them, as God loves them.

Again, depending on the amount of conversation we have, this step needs to take three to six months, so our knowledge, understanding and confidence is improved.

Step 4 - Telling People in Samaria

In Jesus time the Samaritan's believed in God and worshipped God but did not do 'church' the same way as the Jews (which Jesus was).

The Samaritans are those that attend church in other Christian denominations. If we are Baptist, this may be Charismatic, and vice versa. With these conversations, it is important we avoid denominational specifics, as this can cause disagreements, distracting us from our main purpose of talking about God. It is important we understand people can worship differently, and still love and serve God the same.

I learnt this truth in my first year as a Christian. The person who brought me to Christ attended the Church of the Nazarene, the person who gave me my first Bible (which I still have) was a Baptist and the man I worked for, at the time, was Charismatic, spoke in tongues and attended a Catholic church.

The best topics to begin discussions are the same three we've learnt in this book and practiced throughout the previous few steps. The reason for this is to start our talks focused on God, for it is God who changes hearts and minds, not us.

By starting with our focus on God, conversations can drift in many directions and we can often discover the differences, between our denomination and others, are smaller than we may have believed.

Understanding denominational similarities and differences will be an advantage when we begin sharing with non-Christians. If they accept Jesus, we may find they are not comfortable with our way of doing church. If so, they may be more comfortable, and grow more, elsewhere. This concept can be hard for some of us to accept, but the result must always be making Disciples, not increasing our Church's numbers.

Talking with Christians outside our Church gives us another level of growth and confidence, as we again return to the Bible to check the beliefs and thoughts of others. This gives us the ability to move to the last step. Going to the ends of the earth.

Learn
Considering the four steps discussed above, which step do you believe you are currently at? Why?

_____

_____

_____

Think
In each step above, I say you should discuss the first three topics in this book. Why is that important?

_____

_____

_____

_____

Do

Make a list of people you could talk with, from each of the steps above.

Before you move onto the next part of this book, have at least three conversations with others.

_____

_____

_____

_____

Bible reading

Read Acts chapters 2, 3 and 4.

God chat

Ask God for guidance, wisdom and courage to make start conversations. Expect Him to help you, for this is the work He wants all of us to do.

Step 5 - The Ends of the Earth (Sharing with Non-Christians)

This is when most of us believe we move into making Disciples. Which is what we have been taught, but it is far from correct. The process of making Disciples started back at step 1. We have already made at least one Disciple. Ourselves.

Disciples are not Converts. They are far more than that. A Disciple is someone who has accepted Jesus as Savior and Lord AND shares with others about the Good News and love of God. This is something we have been doing since step 2. By sharing with others, we have been teaching them how to do the same, which is a part of making Disciples called Feeding.

Let's now look at the three areas of reaching those who have not accepted Jesus as Savior and Lord.

Farming, Fishing and Feeding

Our collection of skills, knowledge and gifts will allow us to work, as part of God's family, in any, or all, of the three areas of making Disciples.

Farming

In Matthew13:1-23, Jesus talks about the farmer who spread seed, some seeds fell on stony ground and failed to grow, some seeds began to grow but we're choked by weeds and some landed in good soil and grew strong.

Jesus explained the concept in this way, so the average person could understand sharing the Good News of God required going out and doing, regardless of any result we may, or may not see. We can't stay within the four walls of our house or church.

This activity, also described as planting, watering and fertilizing and is a work mainly done for non-Christians, but also has a place for those who are not active (non-practicing) or have gone back into sinful behaviours (backslidden).

We do not have to walk the streets of our town and preach to people to achieve this activity. It is as simple as mentioning God and His love in conversation, or telling others how God has changed our lives, including how, and why, we became a Christian (our testimony).

Of all the things we have learnt through this book, the first section, Identity, is the main concept we want to discuss with those who don't know God. We do this so they gain a positive understanding of God, and the relationship He wants, rather than the negative 'rules and religion' image too many people have.

It is important to remember others don't have to immediately pray the Salvation Prayer (I don't call it the Sinner's Prayer). The people we're sharing with may need two, three or ten others to share, before they are willing to realize how much they need Him. Then the Holy Spirit is the one who will bring them to the Father, not us. Our role is to plant, water and fertilize, which is done by sharing God's Good News and love.

Fishing

Fishers go out with the aim of catching fish. By obeying God's instructions, like they did in Luke 5:4-7 and John 21:4-6, they bring in hauls of fish. These people are often called Evangelists, but anyone called by God, to go out and publicly share the Good News, can have the same result.

Rarely do the words Fishers speak change the hearts of those who don't know God. Almost always, everyone who accepts Jesus as Savior and Lord, has had Christians share with them previously. They have come to God because of the work of those of us who plant, water and fertilize. The Farmers.

Feeding

Feeding is a sharing activity we all can be involved in. Often seen as the least important part of making Disciples, it is the most important.

Despite all the great work of Farmers and Fishers, if no one feeds the new Disciples they will never be able to continue the work of Farming, Fishing and Feeding.

In John 21:15-17 Jesus talks to Peter about looking after the other Disciples.
15When they had finished eating, Jesus asked Simon Peter, "Simon son of John, do you love Me more than these?"
"Yes, Lord," he answered, "You know I love You."
Jesus replied, "Feed My lambs."
16Jesus asked a second time, "Simon son of John, do you love Me?"
"Yes, Lord," he answered, "You know I love You."
Jesus told him, "Shepherd My sheep."
17Jesus asked a third time, "Simon son of John, do you love Me?"
Peter was deeply hurt that Jesus had asked him a third time, "Do you love Me?"
"Lord, You know all things," he replied. "You know I love You."
Jesus said to him, "Feed My sheep."

'Feeding the sheep' is more than providing food to eat, it is teaching people what God is like, what He expects of us, what we can expect in the future and so much more. This is 'feeding' our soul and our spirit. This is what we have been doing throughout the first four steps of Sharing.

Although going to Church, Bible study and prayer group, are important parts of 'feeding', it is also our everyday conversations, it's our words and actions, that show new Christians what living for Jesus is really like. It's being loving and kind and generous. It's talking with and listening to the person standing alone after church. It's visiting someone in hospital (or at their home) when they are ill. It's buying groceries for someone who is struggling. It's being available to share God's love to everybody.

Too often this is left to the Pastor, or church leaders, but are things we can do.

Farming, Fishing and Feeding are all parts of making Disciples. Regardless of our skills, knowledge or gifts there is a part we can play in the greatest work, which is ensuring people get to spend eternity with God.

Learn
Consider the three areas of Farming, Fishing and Feeding. Remember, we never have to be limited to one area. As we grow in confidence, we will find we may work in all three.

Which areas could you be involved in? Why?

_____

_____

_____

Think
Consider the skills and abilities God has given you. How could these be used in the three areas of making Disciples?

_____

_____

_____

_____

Do
Make a list of people in your church who are currently working in the areas you believe you could work in. Now, consider how or when you can approach them to ask how you could help.

Bible reading
Read 1Corinthians chapter 12.

God chat
Ask God for guidance, wisdom and courage to make the first steps into Farming, Fishing or Feeding.

The End and The Beginning

Remember at the beginning of this book I asked a question about your walk with God. Now is when we can answer that question again and compare our answer to our previous one.

My walk with God **after** reading this book is _____ because:

_____

Depending on how our relationship with God was, we could see anything from a minor to a huge change in response.

I want to thank you for joining me on this journey. I hope you gained as much from it as I have.

My prayer is we all take the wonderful things God has taught us and share them with others, helping them to grow as Disciples.

This may be the end of this book, but it is the beginning of a wonderful journey for all of us, as we continue in the life God wants for us.

Until we meet or meet again.

2Corinthians 13:14
May the grace of the Lord Jesus Christ, the love of God, and the fellowship of the Holy Spirit be with you all.

Rod Loader